BARABOO, DELLS, AND DEVIL'S LAKE REGION

LECTOR HOUSE PUBLIC DOMAIN WORKS

BARABOO, DELLS, AND DEVIL'S LAKE REGION

HARRY ELLSWORTH COLE

ISBN: 978-93-5420-256-8

Published: -

LECTOR HOUSE LLP
E-MAIL: lectorpublishing@gmail.com

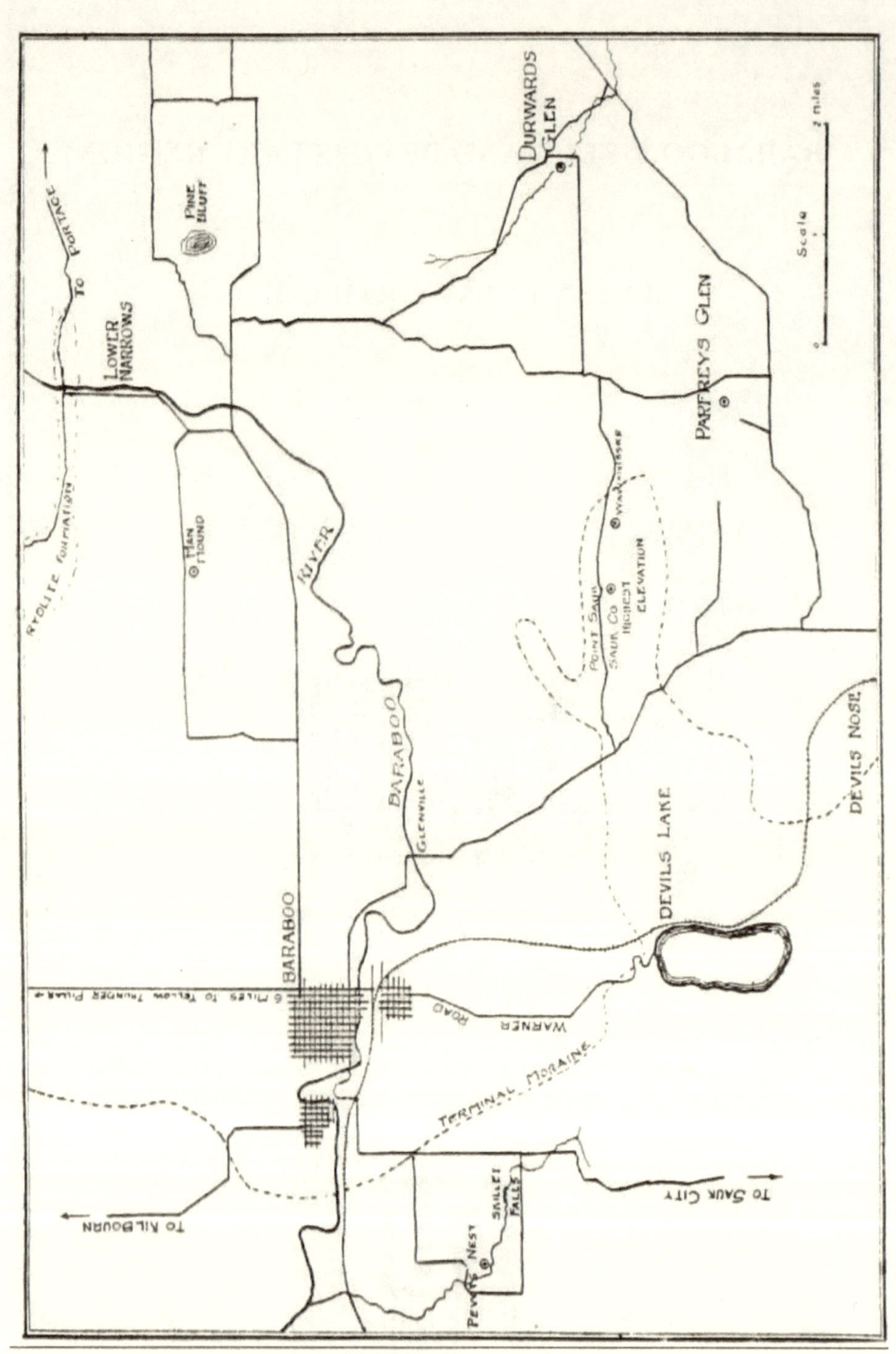

MAP OF THE INTERESTING BARABOO REGION.

BARABOO, DELLS, AND DEVIL'S LAKE REGION

HARRY ELLSWORTH COLE

ISBN: 978-93-5420-256-8

Published: -

LECTOR HOUSE LLP
E-MAIL: lectorpublishing@gmail.com

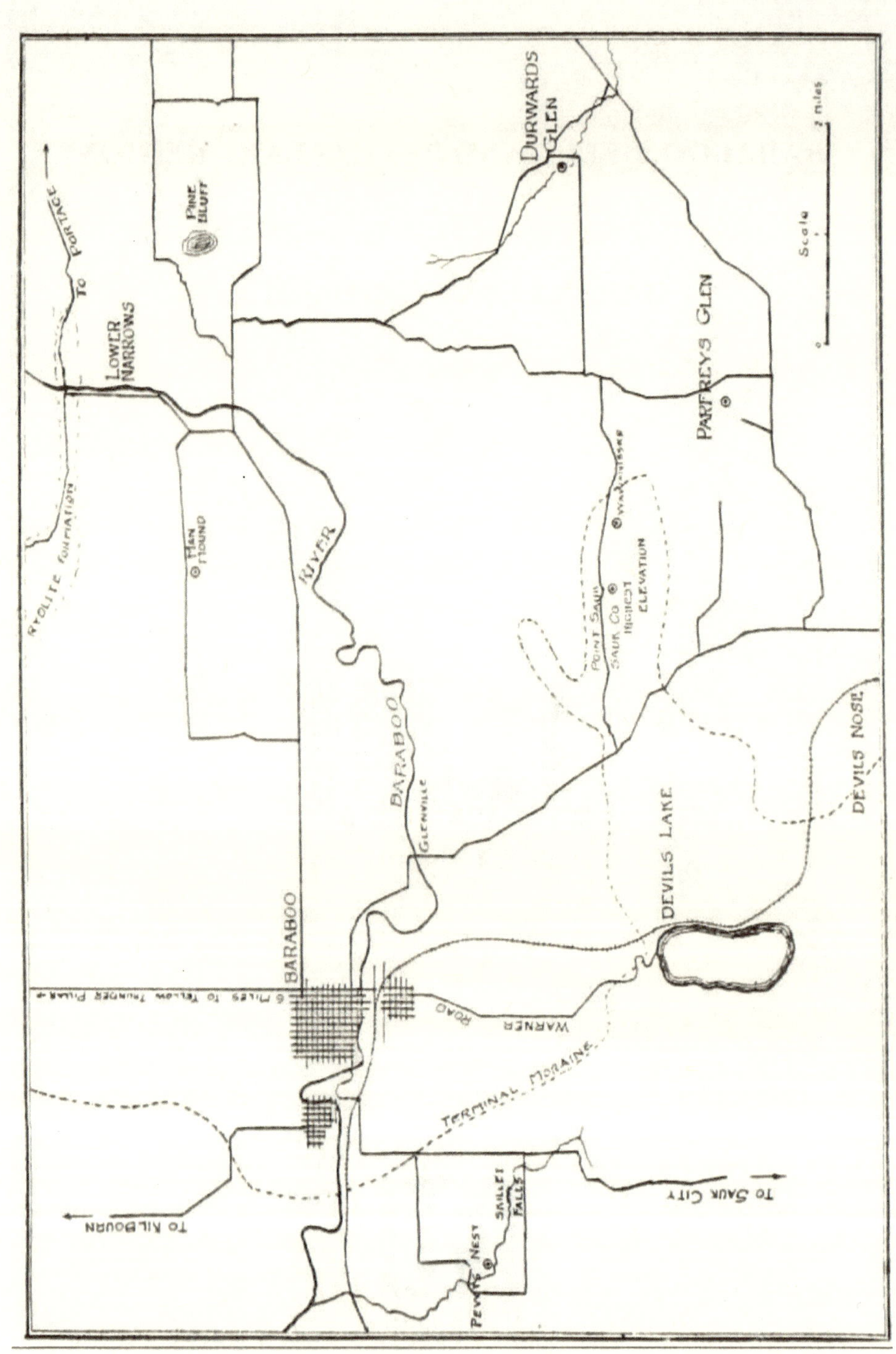

MAP OF THE INTERESTING BARABOO REGION.

BARABOO, DELLS,
AND DEVIL'S LAKE REGION

BY

H. E. COLE

Baraboo. Wisconsin.

WITH MAPS AND ILLUSTRATIONS

FOREWORD

The following pages are intended to give but a faint hint of the geology, archeology, history and scenic beauty of the Baraboo, Dells, and Devil's Lake region. If they add, even in a slight degree, to the pleasure of those who love the out-of-doors, and encourage the local resident as well as the visitor to inform himself concerning the numberless interesting and fascinating features of our countryside, the object for which they were written will have been accomplished.

As to geology, this is a rare field for the student. The igneous rocks, the various formations resting upon them, the drift covered and driftless areas, and the work of erosion through long periods of time have combined to make the region one to which many students are attracted annually.

The Indian earthworks, the village sites, and other relics of a race which once found delight in dwelling here, furnish a rich territory for those interested in the American aborigine.

As to local history, the annals of the white man reach back to 1673 when the first river voyagers went down the Wisconsin. The interesting story is continuous from the days when the region was on the outer rim of civilization to the present time.

Above all is this section rich in natural beauty. The hills and the numerous lakes and rivers have for years attracted tourists from every point of the compass. California and other localities boast greater elevations, larger lakes and more prominent streams, but for unique beauty there are few spots in this country that possess the attraction of the Dells, Mirror Lake, Devil's Lake, and the Baraboo Hills.

In the preparation of these pages valuable assistance in the making of the maps has been given by City Engineer H. E. French of Baraboo and Consulting Engineer W. G. Kirchoffer of Madison. To O. D. Brandenburg, editor of the Madison Democrat, Dr. M. M. Quaife and Miss Louise Phelps Kellogg of the staff of the State Historical Society of Wisconsin, Charles E. Brown, secretary of the Wisconsin Archeological Society, and others the writer is also deeply indebted.

H. E. COLE.

June 1, 1920.

CONTENTS

CHAPTER I

BARABOO—PART I

Origin of Name and First Settlers at Baraboo—Museum—Where
Ringlings First Pitched a Tent

Baraboo, the Gem City, is supposed to have been named for Jean Baribault
(the spelling corrupted into Baraboo), a French trader and trapper who is said
to have bartered with the Indians near the mouth of the stream which bears his
name. First the river was called Baraboo, spelled in various ways, then the name
was applied to the hills, to the city, and to the town.

The city of Baraboo is situated in a boat-shaped valley about twenty miles
in length and of varying width. The north and south range of the Baraboo Bluffs
enclose the valley, the river entering through a gap at the Upper Narrows and escaping through a similar opening at the eastern extremity of the depression.

The first families came to Baraboo about 1840, among them being those of
Eben Peck, Wallace Rowin, and Abe Wood. The water power was the loadstone
that attracted these first settlers, Peck laying claim to the land at the "lower oxbow" and the other two to the power site at the "upper oxbow" of the Baraboo
river. Eben Peck was the first to erect a house in Madison, Mrs. Peck was the first
white woman in the Baraboo valley, and their only daughter, Mrs. A. S. Hawley,
the first white person born in Madison, now resides in the neighboring village of
Delton.

MUSEUM IN COURTHOUSE

The museum of the Sauk County Historical Society in the courthouse contains
many relics of pioneer times and pictures of the pioneers themselves. There are
cases of stone and copper Indian relics; display of badges given by the late Philip
Cheek, at one time department commander of the Grand Army of the Republic of
Wisconsin, by Mrs. Cheek, by C. S. Blanchett and others; number of flintlock and
other old guns; exhibit of polished shells, stalactites, and many very interesting
curios of this locality. The society also possesses a remarkable collection of hand-
made tools.

THE FIRST COURTHOUSE

The first courthouse in Baraboo stood on the north side of the square at about
120 Fourth Avenue. The second story was used by the pioneers, not only for a

courtroom but for church, school, lecture and dancing hall. On one occasion citizens began to arrive for both religious services and a dancing party, there being some mistake in announcing the two events. For a time there was some question as to how the matter would terminate when a violin was brought forth and the floor was soon filled with dancers indulging in the light fantastic. After being deserted by the county officers, and while being used as a saloon, the building was burned on the night of July 4, 1857.

THE AL. RINGLING THEATRE

The beautiful Al. Ringling theatre, 136-140 Fourth Avenue, just west of the old courthouse site, was erected by the oldest of the circus firm of Ringling Brothers on the ground once occupied by the Wisconsin House, the brick portion of which was known in pioneer times as the Little Dutch Tavern. The theatre, a building of unusual beauty, was built in 1915, at a cost of about $100,000. The interior is of French design; instead of a gallery there is a crescent of seventeen boxes above the main floor. The building seats almost 1,000 persons and was opened to the public on the night of November 17, 1915, the owner, then in ill health, being barely able to be present. Mr. Ringling died soon after, January 1, 1916, in the large mansion around the corner to the right.

THE AL. RINGLING RESIDENCE

The Al. Ringling residence of Lake Superior brown stone was erected in 1909, the cost being about $100,000. Here the funeral of a brother, Otto Ringling, was held in 1911. Otto was born in a small frame house that stood about where the north wall of the mansion is located. The only sister of the Ringling Brothers, Mrs. Harry North, and her family now occupy the home.

THE FIRST CHURCH

Across the street to the east of the Al. Ringling residence stood the first church in the Baraboo valley. One winter day in January, 1850, a band of Christian workers cleared away the snow, erected a building 36 by 74 feet from rough boards, filling the spaces between the walls with sawdust, and covering the floor with the same material. A bronze tablet on the treebank marks the site.

AN EARLY COLLEGE

In the days before high schools every village with any pretence to enterprise and enlightenment had a select school or college. The building at the rear of the Ringling residence, 221 and 223 Fifth Avenue, was the home of the Baraboo Collegiate Institute, established in 1858. With the opening of the free high school in Baraboo in the late 60's the institution closed its doors. Originally the building faced the east.

A LITERARY ATMOSPHERE

The street later boasted a literary atmosphere as a little farther to the west, at number 316 Fifth Avenue, lived Jack Boyle, the genial author of the widely read Boston Blackie stories, during the winter of 1919-'20.

LIBRARY WHERE A CHURCH STOOD

Turning to the left at the corner of Fifth and Birch, one block brings the loiterer to the Carnegie Free Public Library, standing on the site of the Free Congregational Church. In the old church Samuel Longfellow, a brother of the New England poet, expounded the doctrines of Unitarianism, the choir singing hymns of his composition. In the same building A. Bronson Alcott interpreted transcendentalism, and Rev. Frederic May Holland, a cousin of Louisa M. Alcott, was heard there.

HOME OF THE GOLLMARS

A little to the south of the library, 507 Birch Street, is the home of the late Mr. and Mrs. G. G. Gollmar, parents of the Gollmar Brothers who owned a circus for many years. The Gollmar sons and daughters are cousins of the Ringlings. The house is now occupied by a daughter, Mrs. Armor Brown.

WHERE THE RINGLINGS FIRST PITCHED A TENT

Turning to the left on Second Avenue one block, then to the right one block, brings the visitor to the county jail, the site where Ringling Brothers first pitched their "big top," May 19, 1884. The old jail stood farther back on the lot and the circus was given near the avenue, the gate of the fence enclosing the grounds standing open all day.

Although they had given hall shows before the first circus performance beneath a tent, that afternoon in May was the beginning of a road which ended in the making of several millionaires.

Across the street and a little to the west, 210 Second Avenue, is where August Ringling (originally spelled Rungeling), the father of the showmen, died in 1898. The family previously lived at number 227, almost at the end of the block on the opposite side of the thoroughfare.

A DREAM OF JUGS

Continuing on Second Avenue one is reminded that on the side of the hill there was once a pottery where jars and jugs were produced in profusion. With the poet one can almost hear the potter sing:

> "Turn, turn, my wheel, turn round and round;
> Without a pause, without a sound."

THE LINCOLN ELM

The large elm in front of the residence at 506 Second Avenue was planted by the late State Senator Frank Avery on the day the news of the assassination of President Lincoln reached Baraboo in April, 1865. It is known as the Lincoln elm.

As with the martyred Lincoln a tragedy came to the tree one day—Jove shot a thunderbolt into its branches, badly injuring it.

NO LIONS NOW

Continuing down the street, the ground to the left and adjacent to the river, was the winter quarters of the Gollmar Brothers' Circus for many years. The circus was established in 1891, was conducted by Charles A., Benjamin F., Fred C., and Walter S., and sold by them in the fall of 1916 to the Patterson Carnival Company.

LARGEST MILL THIS SIDE OF PHILADELPHIA

Across the river stands the Island Woolen Mill (owned by the McFetridge family) the largest plant of its kind west of Philadelphia.

LYONS

Crossing the concrete bridge over the Baraboo River, where the inviting pergolas stand at the ends of the dam, one is in the village of Lyons, platted by W. H. Canfield in 1846, the first plat in the Baraboo valley, and named for Lyons, New York.

Going several blocks to the right after making the first turn, the traveler is on the Baraboo-Kilbourn road. Swinging again to the right the old Indian ford may be seen in the Baraboo River, the highway along the stream occupying the location of an aboriginal trail.

AN EARLY HOME

The log cabin of Wallace Rowin (sometimes spelled Rowan or Rowen) was near the large elm tree by the driveway leading to the residence opposite the ford. Rowin came into the lead region of Wisconsin during the excitement in the 30's, was an early resident at Cross Plains, the first to enter land in Columbia county, and one of the first to come to Baraboo. Rowin, and wife, the first country judge of Sauk county, Lorrin Cowles, his daughter, and others are buried on the ridge of land several rods to the left as one travels a block or more towards Ochsner Park.

THE CITY PARK

The park was acquired by the city in 1918 and formally opened to the public in 1919. The land was purchased from the Ochsner family, the celebrated Chicago surgeon, Dr. A. J. Ochsner, making his interest in the property a gift to the city.

THE FIRST HOUSE IN BARABOO

At the crest of the river bank in the southwest corner of the park is where the first log cabin, the first house, was built in Baraboo. In it lived Abe Wood, his Indian wife, and their two daughters. Wood & Rowin built the first dam in the Baraboo River, a portion of it remaining a few rods below and to the left of where the cabin stood. When the water is low some of the timbers may be seen in the bottom of the stream, placed there in 1840.

AN OLD HOP HOUSE

North of Ochsner Park, on the Dodd estate at 706 Eighth Avenue, stands an old hop house, a reminder of the days when fortunes were made and lost growing the vine in this region.

Leaving the park at the street in front of the brick residence, the old Ochsner home, and continuing on Seventh Avenue to number 617, is found the pioneer homestead of Col. D. S. Vittum, once the scene of much social gaiety. It was a fine place in its day, crowning a hill amongst the forest trees, but like many early American homes, the time has come when it may be said:

"A jolly place in time of old,
But something ails it now."

THE FIRST SCHOOL

At 321 Seventh Avenue, the visitor comes to where the first school was erected in the Baraboo valley. The site was selected by Wallace Rowin, W. H. Canfield, and Lewis Bronson. E. M. Hart the first teacher, resided with his girl wife in the lean-to of the log structure. Notwithstanding an abundance of timber in the immediate vicinity, such economy was exercised in erecting the structure, as a tall citizen once remarked, it was necessary to stoop unusually low when entering the door, "and you could throw a cat through the cracks without touching a hair."

CHAPTER II

BARABOO—PART II

Old Opera House—Cemetery on the Hill—Deserted Ringlingville—
Bunn the Baker of Baraboo

A huge and humorous hoax was the Cardiff Giant. The collapsed humbug was told at every fireside in the land in 1869 and has been retold thousands of times since then. (If the reader is interested go to the Carnegie Free Library, Baraboo, and obtain a copy of the Century Magazine, vol. 64,—new series of Century is Vol. 42—Oct. 1902, page 948; or read in the Sauk County History, 1880, page 547.) The figure was made at Fort Dodge, Iowa, shipped to Chicago, where finishing touches were made, and later taken to Binghampton, New York, then buried on the Newell farm at Cardiff. Not long after the giant was exhumed and still later the fraud was exposed. One of the star actors in the performance was George Hull, who came from Binghampton, New York, to Baraboo, in 1867, and manufactured cigars in a shelly kind of a structure at 614 Oak Street, next to the alley, across the thoroughfare from the rear of the Warren Hotel. While Hull was away the building was burned. It is stated there was insurance of $12,000, that Hull settled for $1,000, and many people said, "Nigger in the fence."

WHERE CELEBRITIES WERE HEARD

At the northeast corner of Oak and Fifth, 701-705, now occupied by a garage, was located the old Opera House. Here were heard such characters as Robert G. Ingersoll, the skeptic; W. J. Bryan, the silver-tongued orator; Elbert Hubbard, a victim on the Lusitania; Opie Read, the author; Robert M. La Follette, the senator; and many others. Nat Goodwin, Salvini and stars of divers magnitude played here and noted musicians filled the structure with their harmonious reverberations. The old building burned on February 22, 1905.

THE OLDEST LIVING THING IN TOWN

If, perchance, one dwells in a town where the inhabitants do not keenly appreciate the pleasure derived from rare old trees, or where the authorities have destroyed many a precious one, the visitor will be charmed with the beauty of the streets of Baraboo. In many places grand old elms arch the thoroughfares, giving wondrous beauty to the vista and shade in the mid-summer season.

The gnarled burr oak nearly opposite the garage, standing at 708 Oak Street, is without doubt the oldest living thing in the town. An appreciative magazine editor once graced the pages of his publication with a story of this old oak and since then it is often spoken of as the "Magazine Tree."

CHURCH WITH MEMORIAL WINDOWS

On the northeast corner of Oak and Sixth Streets is seen Trinity Episcopal Church, a charming edifice of Gothic design, adorned with several memorial windows. A bronze tablet on the interior speaks of the long service of out of the rectors, Rev. Samuel B. Cowdry.

A GIANT OF THE TOWN

A few paces on the opposite side of the street towers a giant cottonwood, one of the largest trees in town. It stands nearly in front of the residence at 821 Oak. Here Mrs. August Ringling, the mother of the circus brothers, enjoyed the evening of life and died in 1907. The daughter, Mrs. Harry North, and her family resided here until the spring of 1919 when they moved to the stone mansion at 617 Broadway.

Diagonally across the way, 107 Seventh Street, is the home of the late J. J. Gattiker, one of the early residents of the town. It is now occupied by his two daughters. This delightful old home, with its luxurious shrubbery and garden, its extensive library and pipe organ, has long been a gathering place for the literary and musical folk of Baraboo.

Passing up the street one block brings the stroller to Eighth, and to the left about two blocks, number 234, is the late home of A. G. Ringling, the first of the seven brothers to answer the call of death. The home is now occupied by Mrs. Ringling.

RELATIVES OF A MOVIE STAR

Just east of the Ringling residence, 218 Eighth Avenue, a small house is half hidden behind a group of pines, the place where Clara Kimball Young's grandparents, Professor and Mrs. J. S. Kimball, resided for many years. The parents of the movie star, Mr. and Mrs. Edward M. Kimball, dwelt there with the professor and his wife for a year or more when the daughter was in her infancy.

OTHER RINGLING HOMES

On up Oak Street, number 103 Tenth, stands the home erected by the late Alf. T. Ringling, who died at Oak Ridge, New Jersey, October 21, 1919. The place is surrounded by a vineclad, sandstone retaining wall, has a commanding view, and is well appointed within. The place is now the home of Mrs. Ringling. Henry Ringling died in September, 1918, in the colonial house at 201 Eighth, erected by Charles E. Ringling and occupied by the family for a number of years. Mrs. Henry Ringling and son now live in the home.

THE BARABOO CEMETERY

One of the pleasing prospects of the region is obtained from the high point on the south side of the Baraboo Cemetery. The burying ground is reached by ascending East Street from the greenhouse, passing the old T. M. Warren home buried among the trees on the right and a row of trees planted on the same side of the thoroughfare through the efforts of the Civic League. The view from the knoll in the cemetery includes a sweep of the eastern portion of the Baraboo Valley and the south range of the Baraboo Bluffs, the Devil's Lake gap being almost directly south and Point Sauk, 1620 feet high, to the southeast. The Baraboo River is hidden in its depressed bed and the lake is closed from view by the terminal moraine left by the sea of ice in glacial times.

In the old cemetery sleep many lawyers, doctors, ministers, merchants, enginemen, trainmen, circusmen, newspapermen, and others identified with the city which is half-hidden below. The mausoleum near the south boundary of the cemetery is that of Henry Ringling, the one farther north and in the same row of lots, that of Al. Ringling. The father and mother and Otto are buried near the granite resting place of the youngest son, Henry. August G. Ringling is interred in St. Joseph's Catholic Cemetery, adjoining the protestant, and near the public highway while Alf. T. sleeps at White Plains, New York.

Between the vault and the sexton's house is the grave of Mrs. Eben Peck, the first white woman to come into the Baraboo Valley, and on a stone in the same lot one reads the name of her son-in-law, Nelson W. Wheeler, the author of "Old Thunderbolt in Justice Court."

THE HULL HOUSE

Returning to the greenhouse and continuing one block south, 820 East Street, one finds where George Hull, of Cardiff Giant notoriety, resided while a dweller in Baraboo.

HOUSE WITH MANY GABLES

While passing Sixth Street one may see on the ridge to the right, number 216 Fifth, the house of many gables. For years the place was the home of Terrell Thomas, the first banker in Baraboo, and here died Rev. Fr. J. T. Durward in September, 1918.

CHURCH WITH BEAUTIFUL WINDOWS

Several blocks towards the river, St. Joseph's Catholic Church stands on the brow of the hill. The structure was erected during the priesthood of the late Fr. J. T. Durward and one of its characteristics is the beautiful windows, impressive and artistic in design, portraying many Biblical scenes.

DESERTED RINGLINGVILLE

At the foot of the hill, and extending several blocks to the eastward along Water Street, lies deserted Ringlingville. For more than thirty years the circus went forth in the spring time and, after a season in many commonwealths, returned with the autumn, weaving into the years a name which will cling to the place for many decades to come. Here the lions roared and the hyenas snarled, while there trumpeted in a building hard by the largest herd of elephants this side of Africa. With the coming of the mellow days of spring, horses and camels and pachyderms in long processions gave to the streets an individual air, while the yards and thoroughfares filled with gilded wagons emphatically denoted the circus center that it was. On account of the war and influenza in the fall of 1918, the show sought refuge in Bridgeport, a calamity in Ringlingville.

A PIONEER HOME

Turning to the west the loiterer passes the Ringling Hotel on the left, and a block more reaches Ash street. Perched on the hill to the right, 308 Ash, is the pioneer home of Colonel D. K. Noyes and family, erected in 1850. It was the first example of a solid and dignified abode in Baraboo, built of red brick and graced with four fluted columns. Between those two same pillars on the left the owner went away to war, losing a foot at Antietam, and to win honors as postmaster and politician. Between those two same pillars the guests assembled on their golden wedding day and later the venerable pair passed out, one after another, to their last resting place on the hill.

BUNN THE BAKER OF BARABOO

Bunn the Baker of Baraboo, made immortal by B. L. T. in the Chicago Tribune, had his shop across the river at 114 Walnut Street, the street name changing at the river. Here the tradesman-merchant with the alliterative appellation, made sweet buns and bread until the fall of 1919 when a home was purchased on Cheek's Hill where Mr. and Mrs. Bunn reside.

BIRDS OF MANY FEATHERS

Advancing and turning to the right on Lynn Street, then crossing the long bridge over the Baraboo River, one arrives at the high school building on the right, and postoffice on the left. In the former structure is the extensive bird collection made by Charles Deininger of Sauk City. Here may be seen a male and female passenger pigeon, mandible to mandible, as if pitifully predicting the doom of the species. At one time millions were slaughtered at roosting places on the bluffs and in the pine woods near Kilbourn, after they had darkened the sky at evening on their return from feeding grounds. At present as far as known no living birds are in existence. The two exhibited are rare and interesting specimens.

AN IDEA MAKES A MILLION

Where the Corner Drug Store is located at the southeast corner of Oak and Third Streets, once stood a frame building fronting the first-named thoroughfare. On the second floor of the old structure A. N. Kellogg published a newspaper and during the Civil war he found it necessary, the typesetter having shouldered arms, to have his paper printed on one side at Madison. The idea developed into the "patent insides" for newspapers. Mr. Kellogg's name became familiar in every rural newspaper office in the land, and he garnered a fine fortune as his reward. His business was absorbed by larger interests several years ago and the name is no longer known in the newspaper world.

CHAPTER III

DEVIL'S LAKE

Devil's Lake State Park—Geology of the Baraboo Hills—The Glacial Epoch—Scenic Wonders

Devil's Lake is one of the outstanding places of beauty and wonder in this region of unusual charm and interest. The placid body of water, with talused slopes and encroaching moraines, is the central object in Devil's Lake State Park, a tract of land containing more than a thousand acres. Few of the visitors who come into this region escape the lure of this wonderful playground.

The Park is reached by traversing three miles of concrete road from Baraboo, the beautiful highway made possible by a bequest of $40,000 by the late W. W. Warner of Madison, an early resident of Baraboo. The contract for building the road was awarded in 1919, the work to be completed in that year and 1920.

AN IRON MINE

Soon after leaving the city, about a quarter of a mile to the right, may be seen a stack of iron ore at the abandoned Cahoon Mine. The mine was opened in 1911 and closed in 1919 after more than a million dollars had been expended. The Baraboo Valley from end to end has been pierced with the diamond drill and iron ore has been found beneath the surface in all the region, often at a depth of 400 feet. Two abandoned mines may be seen southwest of North Freedom and flowing wells here and there tell of the millions expended by various companies in a vain effort to make mother earth yield her riches.

ENTERING THE PARK

Just before entering the Park one's attention is called to the view on the left extending to the Lower Narrows of the Baraboo River and to the Caledonia Hills beyond. Within the Park unique is the vista through the arboreal avenue, rugged rocks on the right and a wooded slope on the left.

The first glimpse of the lake is caught from the terminal moraine, the ridge of land left between the bluffs when the ice was present during the glacial epoch centuries ago. On top of this ridge, toward the railroad track, where the road begins to descend, lies an effigy Indian mound.

GEOLOGICAL WONDER OF THE WORLD

Geologically Devil's Lake is one of the wonders of the world. At the dawn of the earth's history there were no rivers or lakes or bluffs in the Baraboo region, the ocean or an inland sea covering all the land. At the bottom of the sea were the Archean or igneous rocks, the oldest formation known to geology. Upon these rocks the sand was piled a mile deep, the sand at a later time being changed into sandstone and still later metamorphosed into the hard quartzite which towers high in the bluffs. Resting upon the beds of sand were deposits of clay which changed to slate, limestone which became dolomite, and iron which remained in its elemental state.

Balance Rock   View of Devil's Lake   Stone Face

BALANCE ROCK, VIEW OF DEVIL'S LAKE, STONE FACE

Later there was a mountain making movement of the earth and there appeared peaks as lofty as those in the Alps or Rockies. The once horizontal beds of sand, clay, limestone and iron were uplifted and folded in the process, the layers at the lake being inclined about fifteen degrees as seen along the East Bluff. The Baraboo Bluffs are among the oldest formed things on the globe—older than the Rockies or Alleghenies, older than a pound of coal on the earth, older than any tree or bird or beast that ever lived.

There was a long period of erosion and a river cut a gorge through the range where the lake is now located.

In Paleozoic times the sea returned again, the tops of the bluffs stood as islands above the waves, the loose rocks were rounded on the shore, and sandstone almost filled the gorge where there was once a river. The animal life then consisted of trilobites, oyster like organisms, and other low forms.

The sea retreated and a river once more carried away the material which filled the gap in the bluffs. Because the hills of this region were once buried and again exposed to view, they are sometimes called the "Baraboo fossil."

THE GLACIAL EPOCH

Next came the glacial epoch, when the advancing ice from the northeast came into the Baraboo region; this was a long time after the sea retreated the last time, possibly a period of 100,000 or 200,000 years. Into this gorge where probably once flowed the stream we now know as the Wisconsin River, the ice advanced to the terminal moraine, where the visitor descends just before reaching the lake. At the same time another tongue of cold crept into the valley between the Devil's Nose and the Lake. Had the tongues of ice advanced much farther there would have been no lake. Sand and gravel were washed into the gorge, leaving a deposit hundreds of feet thick. The well at the north end of the Lake is 283 feet deep, the drill stopping before it reached the bed of the ancient stream. In times agone the river must have found its way through a chasm 900 or 1,000 feet deep, a scene as picturesque as that of the present gorge below Niagara Falls.

THE LAKE AT PRESENT

The following applies to the lake as it is today:

Above sea level—About 960 feet.

Above the river at Baraboo—About 120 feet.

Height of West Bluff above the lake—About 500 feet.

Height of East Bluff above the lake—A little less than 500 feet near the lake, 610 feet some distance to the east.

Height of South Bluff—At Devil's Nose, 495 feet.

Source of supply—Springs and two small creeks.

Outlet—Evaporation and seepage.

Area draining into the lake—About 5½ square miles.

Greatest length—1¼ miles.

Average width—2,200 feet or ⅖ of a mile.

Greatest depth—43 feet.

Average depth—30 feet.

Circumference—3¼ miles.

Area—388 acres, or ⅗ of a square mile.

Volume at low water—3,495,245,000 gallons.

HISTORY

On the early maps the name of the lake is given as Lake of the Hills. Of it I. A.

Lapham, early Wisconsin traveler and scientist, wrote: "The lake is vulgarly called Devils Lake from the wild, rocky place in which it is found." The Indian name for Devils Lake is Minnewaukan, or Evil Spirit Lake. The lake has unusual echoing powers and for this reason, it is said, the Indians supposed the bluffs to be inhabited by powerful spirits or manitos. The Winnebago have a tradition that the buffalo clan of their tribe had its origin on its shores.

FIRST VISITED

The earliest record of the lake being visited by a white man was about 1839 when James S. Albin, the first permanent settler in Sauk County, came to the bluffs.

CLIMBING THE MOUNTAIN

Between the railroad track and where the path begins its ascent of the East Bluff, stood the Cliff House, a pioneer hotel on the shore of the lake. In the historic structure many a noted traveler tarried, among them Mrs. Abraham Lincoln, and many social events were given; Baraboo folk often mingled with the visitors to the region. W. B. Pearl was the last landlord, leaving the place in 1904. The hotel, annex and other buildings were razed soon after.

ELEPHANT ROCK AND CAVE

The first pause of interest along the scenic, twisting trail, as one ascends the bluff is Elephant Rock. This huge, reclining pachyderm is an unusual freak of nature's chisel.

Just back of Elephant Rock is the Cave, where may be seen some of the quartzite boulders rounded by the waves of the ancient Potsdam Sea. The top of the quartzite, on which the conglomerate rests, is the old sea shore, made smooth by the restless waves of that early time.

Passing onward along the path from Elephant Rock, the pedestrian will see more of the conglomerate as he hugs the cliff, and the fantastic roots twining in and out will not be passed unobserved.

THE TOMAHAWK ROCK

Not far away is Tomahawk Rock, standing erect over the brow of the cliff, just as if placed there by some giant of other times.

Up and down winds the way until a point is reached where the ancient river valley turned to the eastward. Half way down the precipice, you can make it if you are an expert mountaineer, is Balanced Rock, a huge piece of elongated quartzite, shaped much like an inverted dash churn of log cabin days, big at the top and little at the bottom.

From the location of Balanced Rock or from the top of the bluff above may be obtained a rare view of the valley.

DEVIL'S DOORWAY

To the east a few hundred paces is the Devil's Doorway, a quaint arrangement of rocks left as the result of the washing away of the stones and earth through long periods of rain and frost.

ONCE A WATERFALL

Just east of the Doorway the careful observer will find a number of potholes, rounded places in the hard quartzite. These were undoubtedly once in the bed of a river, where a waterfall was an interesting object on the landscape. Potholes can be made in no way except by running or falling water.

Unless the visitor desires to explore the bluffs to the east, the descent is now made a few rods from the potholes. At the upper end of the trail will be noticed a quantity of preglacial gravel about which Professor R. D. Salisbury and William C. Alden and others have written.

Reaching the trees below and keeping close to the rocks, Alaska Grotto will be reached a few rods to the west. If a warm day, go into the depression and feel the flood of cold air pouring outward.

Crossing the railroad track to the shore of the lake, the large bird effigy mound will be noted near the hotel. The length of the body is about 115 feet and the wing-spread about 240 feet. There is a bronze tablet on the mound.

THE WEST BLUFF

On the West Bluff may be seen Cleopatra's Needle, the Turk's Head, and other points of interest. This bluff is often called Palisade Park, so named by A. R. Ziemer who platted a summer city and exploited the place in 1894 and 1895.

The young man died in his cottage in the early winter of 1895 and soon the project fell into decay. The observation tower, his home, the Marsh & Jackson Cottage, and the Coleman place became ruins.

SPRING

Koshawagos Spring, some distance from the southwest corner of the lake, supplies the finest water in the whole locality. It takes its name from the Koshawagos Club House hard by, the word meaning "Men of the Valley."

THE INDIAN MOUNDS

Besides the animal effigy on the north terminal moraine and the bird near the Kirkland Hotel, the following may be mentioned: a low mound west of the Cliff House site cut by the railroad: two linears about thirty rods to the west, one extending into the public road; and the Terminal Moraine group in front of the Claude Cottage. A bear effigy, a linear and still another effigy are quite plainly outlined while two others are almost obliterated.

Nestling near the west bluff is the late home of L. W. Claude, who came from

Ambleside, England, to the Lake in pioneer times. The rugged beauty of the spot recalled the charm of his former home in the fascinating lake region and, with his family, he enjoyed the Lake for many years. The interesting home is now occupied by the family only during the summer seasons.

MUCH FOR THE BEHOLDER

These ragged rocks and towering cliffs are most overpowering when viewed from a boat coasting along the western shore of the lake.

An adequate description of this picturesque spot is not attempted here. The life in the lake, the ferns and flowers on the slope, the fur-coated and feather-covered friends in the wood, as well as the charm of the Lake itself in its unusual environment, are left for the enjoyment of the visitor. Nor has anything been said of Indian legends which hover over the lofty crags and cling to the rocky shores.

"The mountain's wall in the water,
It looks like a great blue cup,
And the sky looks like another,
Turned over, bottom side up."

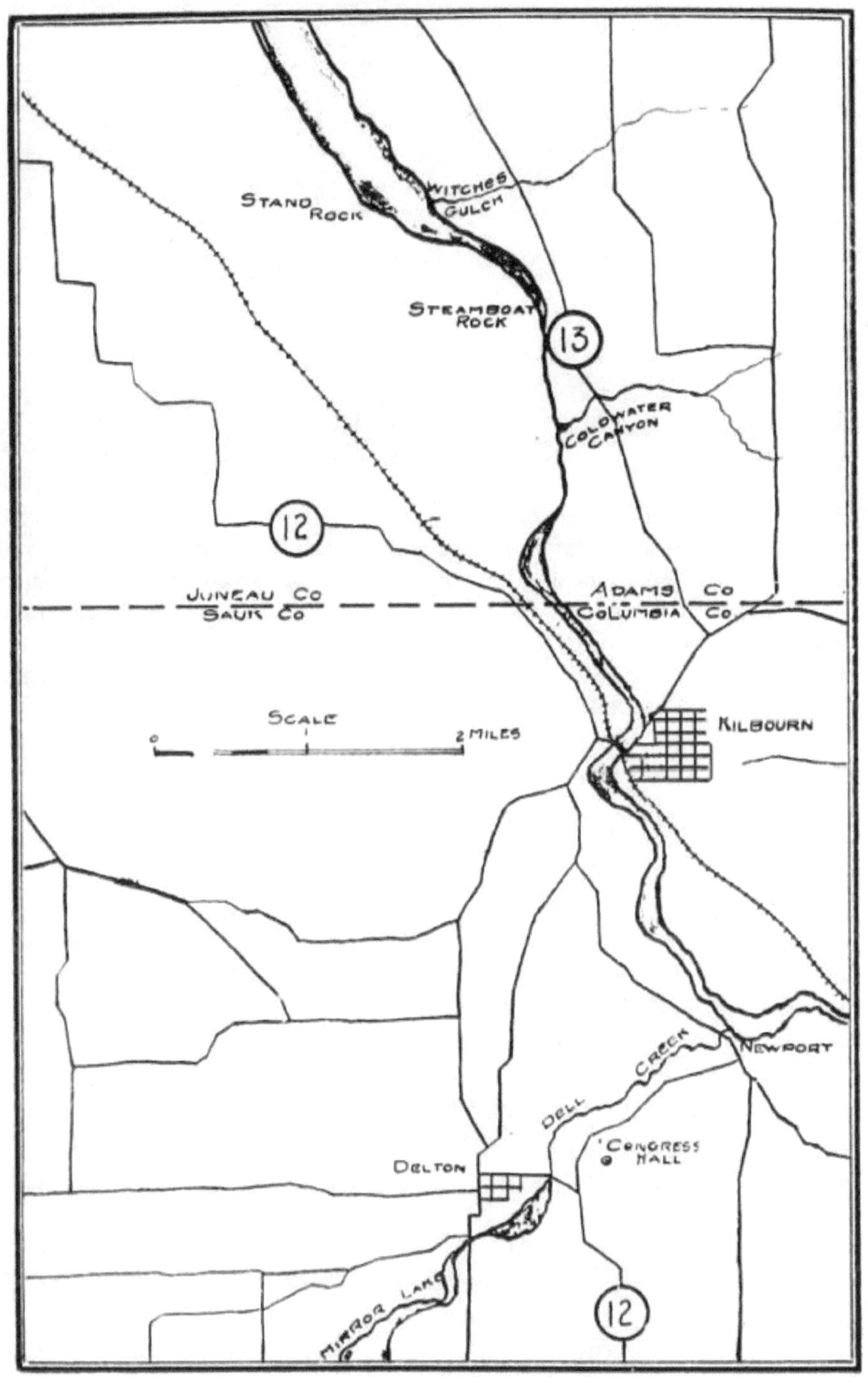

THE DELLS AND MIRROR LAKE REGION

CHAPTER IV

WISCONSIN RIVER DELLS

Wisconsin River Dells—Journey of Fascinating Scenery—Jefferson Davis—Belle Boyd, Rebel Spy

No portion of the Badger state is more widely known for scenic beauty than the Wisconsin River Dells. Each passing year thousands of persons revel in the charm of this region, often remaining throughout the summer enjoying the hospitality of the city of Kilbourn, which is picturesquely located on the bank of the river. Here the stream has cut a great gorge through the sandstone rocks leaving wonderful castellated crags standing high on either side and fascinating niches below through which the water bubbles and boils in caldrons of solid rock. Shaded pathways invite the visitor to explore fern-hung nooks that hold especial interest for the botanist and the vari-colored sands and rocks possess unusual attractions for those interested in unique geological formations.

THE WAY FROM BARABOO

From Baraboo to the Dells, the way is over Trunk Line No. 12. The road first climbs the north range of the Baraboo Bluffs, then crosses Webster's Prairie, the terminal moraine, relic of the ice epoch, forming the sky-line along the way, less than a mile to the east. This extensive prairie, a veritable flower garden in the days before the first plow-share disturbed the soil, is the outwash from a wall of glacial ice that, during the ice epoch, extended for miles in a northerly and southerly direction near the site of the present highway. It is now the center of a prosperous rural community.

THE MARSHALL FARM

Some eight or nine miles distant from Baraboo, shortly before the road turns to the left, an interesting old residence is observed, The Elms, the home of the Marshall family, early residents of the Prairie. The place, which once included 1,476 acres, is owned by Judge R. D. Marshall of Madison, for many years a member of the supreme court of the state. The acreage has been somewhat reduced in recent years.

From the Marshall farm the road pursues a winding way, crossing Dell Creek and passing through the sequestered village of Delton where it turns abruptly to the right following an almost continuous avenue of pines into Kilbourn.

THE DELLS

The way to see the Dells is by boat. Throughout the entire length of the narrow passage a fanciful nomenclature adds to the romantic character of the objects and places. Before the great dam was built at Kilbourn a number of peculiarly interesting points, now buried by the whirling waters, were exposed to view. The erection of the dam, although destroying these particular features, has added to the uniqueness of others, resulting as a whole in increased attractiveness for the Dells.

THE NARROWS, DELLS OF THE WISCONSIN

One hundred feet deep. The river seems almost to be running on its edge hemmed in by ponderous rocks.

Courtesy Wisconsin Geological Survey

The points of interest usually called to the attention of visitors by the guides follow:

Angel Rock on the right is a rugged projection, curiously shaped. The imagination will easily transform this lofty crag into a huge angel with outspread wings. It is sometimes called Marble Rock, from the rounded sandstone pebbles on the ledge and in the river.

The Swallow's Home is where the swallows live. During the nesting season thousands of these birds may be seen occupying innumerable holes in the side of the cliff.

The Jaws of the Dells, the entrance proper, are guarded by High Rock and Romance Cliff, two immense rocks standing as sentinels to the waterway.

Chimney Rock is one of nature's freaks, resembling a stick and mortar chimney of pioneer times. It was fashioned by the waters as they cut this wonderful gorge.

Echo cove is submerged.

Black Hawk's Head is another curious result of erosion.

Nothing but the site is left of the ancient and weathered Dell House, once a "wild, rambling old rookery." It was the first frame house built on the river above Portage, erected in 1837-38 by Robert V. Allen and used for many years as a tavern. Here the rivermen recounted their thrilling experiences in piloting their rafts through the Dells and told of the days in the pineries of pioneer Wisconsin.

Chapel Gorge is a beautifully shaped glen on the right, named for a peculiarly shaped rock at the entrance.

Boat Cave is submerged.

Circle Bend is a half-circle in the river, the cliff of solid masonry formed of rocks high and bold.

Sturgeon Rock resembles the fish by that name. It is located on the left at the entrance to the wild grandeur of the Dells.

The Navy Yard exhibits the geological formation of the Dells in the superlative degree. Huge vessels with prows and sides and ribs of solid stone, may be pictured without difficulty by the imagination, all warring with the waters of the narrows.

Opposite the Navy Yard is Eaton Grotto, a long deep opening in the face of the cliff.

Skylight Cave is submerged.

At the Narrows the river is only fifty-two feet wide, but over 80 feet deep. Here the stream runs on its edge, hemmed in by ponderous rocks. In 1850 Schuyler S. Gates built a bridge over the stream at this place, the first ever thrown across the Wisconsin River. After thousands of teams and passengers had paid toll, the high water of 1866 carried it away.

The Devil's Elbow marks the place where the stream makes a square turn as it enters the Narrows.

Black Hawk Cave on the left, so lingers a legend, is where the chief secreted himself after his disastrous war of 1832.

Notch Rock, near the water's edge, was the terror of raftsmen, more than one raft breaking up and more than one life being lost at this place.

Artist's Glen, on the right, is one of the most beautiful retreats of the Dells.

Sliding Rocks, at the edge of the water, are so named from their peculiar formation, apparently sliding inward and throwing the water to the center of the stream.

The Ancient River Bed is seen on the left. In an early day a portion of the river flowed through the now deserted channel, entering the main stream near the Dell House site and forming an island.

Coldwater Canyon is one of the grand features of the Dells. This is a rocky defile with frowning crags and perpendicular walls.

The Devil's Jug, thirty-five feet across at the bottom and seventy feet high, is a never-ending wonder.

The Devil's Arm Chair is submerged.

The Clam Banks are just above, a place in name only.

The Ruffle Rocks adorn the side of the stream.

Chameleon Cave, with beautiful changing mosses, is near Steamboat Rock.

Steamboat Rock, without smoke-stack and wheel-house, challenges attention.

Roods' Glen is on the right.

Honey Bee Spring is submerged.

Arch Cove gives a view of the river above.

Witches' Gulch is of rare interest and extends for three-quarters of a mile from the shore.

Above Witches' Gulch are the Hornets' Nest, Luncheon Hall, Stand Rock, Demon's Anvil, Louis Bluff and Elephant Back. All around is a panorama of beauty.

JEFFERSON DAVIS AT DELLS

In pioneer times, before the day of the tourist, with each returning vernal season a procession of rafts passed through the Dells. There was no dam below in those days and the surging waters carried more than one raft to destruction and more than one raftsman to his doom. Among the first timbers to be floated through the gorge was lumber for the building of Fort Winnebago at Portage, cut on the Yellow River by Jefferson Davis and a detail of soldiers. It is said the future president of the Southern Confederacy rode one of the rafts through the surging waters to its destination many miles below.

OTHER ATTRACTIONS

Besides the Dells there are other places of interest at beautiful Kilbourn.

The hydro-electric dam and power station is within easy walking distance of the boat landing.

There is a small museum in the library building, which is situated a short distance east of the business section of the village.

One block east of the library and one block to the right a number of deer may be seen in a park owned by J. Wirtz.

Miss Anna Kriegel, taxidermist, has a collection of birds of the region. Her home is a short distance north of the fairground.

Taylor Glen and Tunnel, Rocky Arbor, and Indian Cavern are within easy reach.

In the Kilbourn State Bank may be seen a collection of Indian relics, the property of L. N. Coapman, the cashier.

GRAVE OF REBEL SPY

The grave of Belle Boyd, the noted Rebel spy, is in the Kilbourn Cemetery, her resting place being south of the center and near the Maybee monument. She was born in Martinsburg, West Virginia, in 1846. When a girl she heard the federal troops were threatening her "beloved south" and galloped at night to Stonewall Jackson to convey to him the news. Soon after she was captured and taken to Washington where she became a favorite through her charming manners. After being in prison for a time, she was exchanged for Colonel Michael Cochoran of the Irish Brigade.

Not long after her boldness brought her into the custody of the federal troops again and this time she was ordered to be shot, but was banished. Once more she was captured, once more ordered shot, and once more ordered banished by President Lincoln. Then she went to London where she married Lieutenant Harding who had once caused her capture, creating an international sensation. After his death she married again and after the demise of her second husband wedded Mr. High at Detroit. While with a theatrical company in Kilbourn in 1900, death unexpectedly came and now with each returning Memorial Day flowers are placed upon her tomb by Northerners—those whom she risked her life to oppose.

INDIAN MOUNDS

About three miles southeast of Kilbourn where the highway crosses the Chicago, Milwaukee & St. Paul Railroad tracks, there are a number of Indian mounds. The first of these, the Crossing Group, consists of six conical mounds on an elevation near the road at the river crossing. Across the creek to the south and near the highway is a conical mound and along the river bank, quite close to it, other mounds may be seen, the last holding a commanding view on the high bank. The cultivated land between the farm house and railroad track shows evidences of having been a village site.

Rattlesnake Rock is a high crag on the left.

In the woods east of the Crossing Group are fifteen earthworks, two effigy, three linear, and ten oval or burial mounds. These are known as the Gale Group, for Miss Hattie Gale of Kilbourn.

Partly in a cultivated field and partly in the woods to the northeast may be seen the Bennett Group, named for the late H. H. Bennett of Kilbourn. He it was who made the Dells widely known through his wonderful photography. Of these Indian memorial the most striking mound in the group is a bird (north side of the woods) having a wing spread of 295 feet.

Between the Crossing Group and Kilbourn are two mounds on the Ole Helle place.

MURDER IN THE HIGHWAY

Early one morning in the autumn of 1869, the body of Schuyler S. Gates was found under the trees by the side of the highway, about forty rods from where the Lyndon road leaves the highway leading to Baraboo, less than a mile southeast of the railroad structure over the river at Kilbourn. The spot is just east of the bridge which spans the little creek flowing through the valley into the Wisconsin below the dam. The killing of Gates was laid at the door of Pat Wildrick, a notorious desperado of the neighborhood, then confined in jail. His pal, Perry Richardson, twenty-seven years afterward, was arrested for the shooting of Gates, but he was not tried because there were no witnesses to appear against him. Not long after the cruel murder of Gates, while Wildrick was confined in the jail at Portage, a band of men one night gained entrance by a ruse and the next morning, as expressed by J. C. (Shanghai) Chandler, the prisoner was hanging from a tree in such a way that he could not wipe his nose.

CHAPTER V

LOWER DELLS—DESERTED VILLAGE

Lower Dells—Site of a Deserted Village—Indian Earthwork—Where
They Danced—Woodland Walk

Not so picturesque as the Upper Dells, nevertheless interesting, the Lower Dells extend two or three miles below the hydro-electric plant at Kilbourn. The river is broader and the rocks have been cut away to a greater extent, leaving them hollowed and worn into many shapes. The most fantastic forms are far down the stream. The Lower Dells may be visited by boat or may be carefully examined by walking along the shore in the vicinity of the deserted village of Newport.

In the order of their appearance, the objects of interest are met, as one descends the river, as follows:

Echo Point is where Taylor's Glen is crossed by the railroad and, standing at the mouth of the tunnel, one may hear his voice come back as a boomerang out of space.

Bear's Cave is a recess a little lower on the same side of the river.

Chimney Rock much resembles the one in the Upper Dells, except for size, and is located just below Bear's Cave.

Pulpit Rock is at the water's edge hard by.

Observation Point gives a view of a magnificent landscape.

Stultz Rock, on the opposite side of the stream, was a terror to raftsmen, their craft often being whirled to destruction at this treacherous location.

The Hawk's Bill boldly exposes itself to view, the point being known for many years as Signal Peak.

The Sugar Bowl, Inkstand, and Lone Rock stand amid the swirling waters of the stream, boldly battling with the forces of erosion. They are hard cores which have been left as the river cut its way to the present level.

The Cave of the Dark Waters, called by the Indians, Nah-huh-nah, is an interesting place for the boat to pause.

Grotto Rock and other places of interest will be pointed out by the boatman as the craft glides along.

A DESERTED VILLAGE

Newport, once a noisy, busy place, boasting of two thousand frontiersmen, and now a deserted village site with but a few cellar holes to recall its past glory, was located where the highway, extending east from Delton, joins the Wisconsin River road. The pioneer village was at the head of navigation, this being given as the excuse for its appearance, and after an ephemeral existence of but a few years, passed so completely from view that little remains but a ghostly recollection of the place.

Here the rivermen found a breathing place when they re-assembled their rafts after running the cribs through the gauntlet of the Dells, here the river steamers halted to unburden their cargoes and assume new responsibilities for the downward trips; and here the overland stages drew up at the great Steele tavern to enable the passengers to set foot on the new El Dorado. There was first a limited village plat which included a few blocks, but as the excitement grew, divisions and sub-divisions were added until there was danger of engulfing the village of Delton and even the cemetery two or three miles away. Those with a speculative turn, far and near, purchased lots and blocks in the upstart town, only to have the castle of disappointment fall about their ears.

One day the gasconading inhabitants wore an expression of assurance, the railroad, then approaching, would cross the river into their very midst, and some of them did not hesitate to place fabulous valuations on their property, but ere they were aware land had been purchased where Kilbourn is located and a rival village sprung up almost in a night, dashing the hopes of those residing in Newport. When the railroad was built on the other side of the river, their spirits went to the very depths. An effort was made to revive the hopes of those with homes there, and one night there was a real "resurrection." Speeches were made in defiance of the railroad magnates who dared to attempt to obliterate their existence, songs were sung to cheer the crestfallen, and a mammoth cake, blazing with many candles, graced the banquet board.

All efforts were without avail, however, and it was not long before there was a procession of buildings moving like prehistoric monsters across the landscape, to Kilbourn and elsewhere. Where there was much dancing and delight there is now naught but an air of desertion and dreams.

Although Newport is as dead as Caesar's ghost, much remains of interest. North of the bridge which spans Dell Creek are clumps of lilac bushes, flanking half-filled cellar holes, where once stood pioneer homes, the lilacs persisting since the disaster to the village in the late sixties. Trees have taken possession of the main street of the town, and where the proud villagers once discussed their fortunes and misfortunes, there is slumberous delight.

Near the crest of the elevation in the woods about equally distant from the river, bridge, and highway, is a cave where the brewer stored his bibulous product for the intemperate tipplers. The chiseled cavity in the sandstone rock persists to this day.

A beautiful walk leads to the north, following the river bank, once frequented by rivermen, and no doubt by Indians, as they threaded the trail in early times.

Over on the highway to the left, a quarter of a mile from the Dell Creek bridge, stands "Dawn", the old Vanderpool residence, remodeled by the late S. H. Kerfoot of Chicago. It is the only home remaining in that section of the village.

Passing the bridge or other favored spots on the shore, one may see fishermen contentedly waiting for a pickerel or pike oblivious to the passing of time and the passer-by.

INDIAN EARTHWORK

At the rear of one of the cottages south of the bridge may be seen an Indian mound of the lizard type. It has survived the trials and tribulations of this interesting place.

A few rods to the south, at the rear of other cottages, a linear mound may be seen. (As to why mounds were built see chapter on the Man Mound.)

As previously noted, the Steele Tavern stood where the road from Delton joins the main highway. This was one of the famous frontier places of entertainment for travelers, journeying by stage or prairie schooner from Milwaukee to La Crosse. For many years, long after the last inhabitant had reluctantly left Newport, the homely hostelry defied wind and weather until decay was devouring in every part. Although many had become accustomed to the landmark for a generation or more, it was no doubt a relief to all when it was pulled down and carted away.

WHERE THEY DANCED

During the hop-growing times of the mid-sixties, pickers took possession of the rambling, old tavern, using it to protect them from inclement weather and as a place for frolicsome dances after the day's duties were done. Here resounded the violin, and the prompter's voice, above the music and gliding feet, was heard, in the quadrille, "The Girl I Left Behind Me," to sing—

> "First couple lead to the right,
> Stop right there and balance;
> Pass right through and balance, too,
> And swing with the girl behind you.
> Right and left four."

A WOODLAND WALK

A few rods to the southeast from the cottages, over a stile or two and across a ravine, runs a road through the deep woods. Here one finds a delightful walk of a little less than a mile, traversing the arboreal slope, the sandy river bed, and a weathered rock which, at flood-time, is an island in the stream. From a projecting point one obtains a view of the Sugar Bowl, the Inkstand, and other delights of the Lower Dells.

Just south of the wooded road, at no great distance from the cottages, a bald hill lifts itself above the surrounding landscape, richly rewarding one if he decides to gain its treeless crest.

BRIDGE ACROSS DELL CREEK

Although Newport was a noisy, busy place, crowded with adventurers seeking the gold at the foot of the elusive rainbow, stirred with martial music as the soldiers of the sixties drilled on the Vanderpool green and departed for southern conflict fields, alive with the rivermen who came and went with the departing of each vernal season, the past gives an emphasis to the stilness that broods over it today.

No wonder summer cottagers seek the quiet here. The lingering associations, the pleasant pathways, the changing river, with summer clouds floating across the sky are fascinations not to be painted in words.

COLDWATER CANYON

(Upper Dells.)

SUGAR BOWL

(Lower Dells.)

CHAPTER VI

MIRROR LAKE—CONGRESS HALL

Mirror Lake, Retreat of a Circusman—Earlier Bed of Dell Creek—
Congress Hall Near Village

At the edge of the village of Delton, ten miles north of Baraboo, on Trunk Line 12, Dell Creek once flowed unhampered through a narrow canyon of unusual beauty. When a dam was thrown across the slender stream, a lovely lake, whose placid bosom mirrors daily the changing verdure of its banks, was created, some three miles in length. Boatmen make regular trips on the lake, always before nightfall as the narrow course requires expert piloting. So quiet are the waters that every detail of sky and shore and passing craft are reflected therein; often there is not a ripple, not a cat's paw to mar the mirror. The banks, which are high and rocky, are covered with a dense growth of pine, cedar, hemlock and many other varieties of timber. Underneath is a wonderful carpet of ferns and wild flowers from the meshes of which occasional rabbit or squirrel emerges, or the drumming of a partridge is heard, to divert the attention.

Many cottages are hidden among the trees, but a few being visible from the water's edge. Most of them have an outlook over the lake but are not easily discerned through the wealth of foliage. Occasionally one is seen perched on an outstanding rock, thereby gaining a charming view of the lake. The resinous atmosphere created by the heavy growth of pine is particularly refreshing to the city dwellers who come to this lake in increasing numbers, season after season. The slopes of the lake are the home of the trailing arbutis whose delicate pink blossoms, half hidden, half exposed, are eagerly sought by visitors in early spring.

Of cultivated land one sees but little, and that in the hazy distance. The axe has remained at a respectful distance from the shore, leaving the slopes native clad.

The best fishing grounds are where the lake throws an arm to the left, as one ascends the wild watery defile. Usually one may see disciples of Walton grasping their rods, indifferent to the torrid sun or drenching rain. The patient anglers cast their lines right and left, frequently luring an unsuspecting bass or smaller fry from the undisturbed depths.

Before glacial ice covered a great portion of Wisconsin, Dell Creek probably flowed in a southeasternly direction through a gap in the north range of the Baraboo Bluffs and emptied into the Baraboo River at Baraboo. Its old bed being filled, in a manner similar to the Wisconsin River at the Dells, it was forced to seek a new course and cut a canyon through the sandstone formation.

PLACES OF INTEREST

A ride from end to end brings into view the following interesting features:

The Devil's Postoffice is in a recess at the mouth of a ravine.

The Devil's Five Fingers are all that is visible of a sunken tree. The limbs have been protruding from the water for almost half a century.

SCENE AT MIRROR LAKE

Echo Rock is a high promontory on the left, a distinct echo being heard opposite this interesting feature.

Fern Dell is one of the most attractive places in the whole region.

The narrow valley, with overhanging crags and luxuriant verdure, astonishes the beholder.

RETREAT OF GREAT CIRCUSMAN

The erection of a commodious hotel in Delton by Mrs. Eliza Ringling, adds to the convenience of those desiring to visit the popular resort. Mrs. Ringling's late husband, Al. Ringling, eldest of the circusmen, spent many delightful days in his cottage in the woods at the upper end of this attractive inland body of water.

CONGRESS HALL

A short distance east of the village of Delton, on the south side of the highway leading to the Wisconsin river, is Congress Hall. Here a rivulet has cut a ravine, much of the work evidently having been done in times long past, when there was more water than at present flowing along the course. Early in the spring a creek finds its way through the narrow gorge, but in late summer, after the May showers and June rains have passed, one may explore the elongated, eroded canyon without inconvenience from moisture. The Hall is wildly broken and much distorted in its windings. Often there are spacious openings as if for rooms, narrow passages leading into other chambers sufficiently ample for a congress to gather. These views are quite different from others in the region and will well repay a visit.

CHAPTER VII

PEWIT'S NEST—SKILLET FALLS

Pewit's Nest Near Baraboo—Home of a Recluse—Skillet Falls—
Graves of Napoleon Soldiers

But a trifle over three miles from Baraboo, in the early 40's, a queer enigmatical character secreted himself in the rocky recesses of Pewit's Nest. To this wildering abode he unexpectedly came, lived for a time, and mysteriously disappeared like a phantom or will-o'-the-wisp.

After rumbling over the bridge at the Island Woolen mill, climbing the curved incline, and passing over the viaduct above the railroad tracks, the course to Pewit's Nest follows the main highway which turns here to the right for a half a mile and another half mile to the left. Leaving the main road, No. 12, the course follows a mile to the right climbing the terminal moraine and crossing the outwash plain—and still another half mile to the left the journey brings the visitor to a little rural school-building by the roadside, the place to abandon the car. Here Skillet Creek has cut a wide-mouthed valley or pocket, Pewit's Nest being a quarter of a mile to the left of the main road.

Sward-sided cellar holes are all that remain of a few rude dwellings built about a primitive mill. At one time the jaws at the mouth of the Nest supported a great iron shaft, a cumbersome overshot waterwheel deliberately delivering the contents of the creek, by means of its buckets, into the pool below. In the process logs were converted into lumber, a painfully tedious operation.

A QUEER ABODE

Before building the mill, however, there dwelt in a recess of the solid sandstone, an ingenious and eccentric character whose presence and unusual behavior gave the name to the place. In his "Outline Sketches" W. H. Canfield, local historian, who located on Skillet Creek in 1842, says the abode of this individual was ten feet above a deep pool of water, dug out by the fail of the creek over the crest of the resisting formation. The approach to this nearly secreted habitation was either through a trap door in the roof, or a trap-door in the floor. If one entered through the roof it was by clambering down the rocky wall to the opening, and if through the floor it was by means of a floating bridge upon the pool, a ladder at its end leading to the trap-door in the floor. The little shop could not be seen from the mouth of the canyon, or from the top, or from any direction but one, hence by the early settlers was dubbed the "Pewee" or "Pewit's Nest."

Here the recluse repaired watches, clocks, guns, and occasionally farming utensils, even essaying to manufacture the latter in a rude way. Lathes he had for turning iron and wood, the power for propelling being provided from an old fashioned centrifugal water wheel, itself as much of a curiosity as its owner. A large coffee mill, likewise a grindstone, was arranged to operate by the water that was forever collecting in the upper valley and pouring through the shady dell. It is said that this hermit of the hill could tell a lively tale and dispelled the gloom of loneliness by playing upon a violin. At times, forsooth, he was persuaded to preach for the Mormon church, although his activities in this direction were never pronounced. Among his other accomplishments, he posed as a doctor and prescribed as remedies the herbs and shrubs growing in the valleys and on the hills about.

His favorite place of abode seems to have been the border of a new country and when the settlements among the Baraboo Bluffs became too numerous, he as quietly and mysteriously disappeared from his queer home at Pewit's Nest as he had come.

SKILLET FALLS

Skillet Falls is located about a mile above where the stream tumbles into the pool at the head of the peaceful valley and may be reached by following the creek through woods and fields, or by approaching through the farmyard of Dwight Welch on Trunk Line 12. This place of interest was named by Levi Moore from the "Skillets" or water-worn holes in the sandstone rock, looking much like basins or iron vessels used in cooking.

STREAM WITH TWO BEDS

Before the time of the glacial epoch Skillet Creek probably emptied into the Baraboo River where the city of Baraboo is located, two or three miles below the present confluence. The moraine material filled a portion of the bed of the stream and after the ice receded it was forced to find a new course near where three roads meet, a short distance above Skillet Falls. The upper portion of Skillet Creek tumbles down the Baraboo Bluffs over a bed which dates to Potsdam times while the lower portion is of much more recent origin, something unusual in the history of streams. This interruption in its career has resulted in the picturesque waterfalls. From the highway east of Skillet Creek one has a view of the terminal moraine to the east and of the highly productive outwash plain.

SKILLET FALLS

MARCHED WITH NAPOLEON

Continuing on the highway a mile west of Pewit's Nest one observes a rural burying ground on the slope of Rock Hill. A little south of the center in Rock Hill Cemetery sleep two soldiers who marched with Napoleon in his world-disrupting European conquests. On a marble stone one reads:

```
*     * * * * * * * * * * * * *     *

*     Michael Hirschinger    *

*            Died            *

*       March 20, 1853       *

*        Age 67 Years        *

*     * * * * * * * * * * * *     *
```

The father of former Assemblyman Charles Hirschinger, this soldier's most thrilling experience was his march to Moscow in the fall of 1812 and his retreat with the great Corsican. Half a million men marched triumphantly into the beautiful city, only to have it reduced to ashes in their very presence. This meant the destruction of Napoleon's army. The soldier often retold the retreat through the Polish snows, recalling that some of his comrades, after crossing streams, perished in the snow.

The tomb of Mrs. Hirschinger is near that of her husband.

Near the grave of Michael Hirschinger one reads on a stone about all that is known of still another Napoleon soldier:

```
*     * * * * * * * * * * * * *     *

*       Michael Nippert      *

*            Died            *

*        May 23, 1864        *

*   Age 70 Years, 2 Months   *

*     * * * * * * * * * * * *     *
```

As to his martial deeds but little is recorded. By his side sleeps his wife.

Napoleon went to St. Helena; Hirschinger and Nippert came to the Baraboo Hills.

HIRSCHINGER SPRING

A mile and a quarter south of the cemetery, where the road bends to avoid plunging into it, a spring of delicious water bursts from the hillside and escapes into the quietude of a wooded dale. This obscure valley is known as Pine Hollow and the tortuous streamlet, which finds its way for almost a mile through the towering timber of this delightful retreat, is known as Pine Creek. Ferns, mosses, and certain varieties of wild flowers hide the gray of the rocks which are piled high above the stream. The dale is one of great attractiveness to a loiterer through this unfrequented wood of the Baraboo Hills.

CHAPTER VIII

MAN MOUND, INDIAN EARTHWORK

Man Mound, Famous Archeological Wonder—Why Indian Earthworks Were Built

The famous man mound, a few miles northeast of Baraboo, is the most interesting archeological feature of the region. This earthwork is shaped like a giant
human figure and is the only known Indian monument of this nature in the world.

A DEER MOUND

On the way to the site of the man mound, a deer mound may be visited at 727
Eighth Street, Baraboo, (on Trunk Line 33, Baraboo to Portage) in an oak grove, on
land owned by Mrs. Catherine Crandall Train. The rear portion of this mound, a
rare effigy, was destroyed a number of years ago. A linear mound may be seen just
back of the effigy.

Continuing on the trunk line two miles, a turn is made to the left, the highway
approaching a rugged elevation on the left side of the road. This outcrop of sandstone is known locally as Rocky Point or Violet Hill, from the abundance of violets
which carpet its slopes in the spring. Violent Hill would perhaps be a better appellation as the point has been responsible for a number of serious accidents. Early in
the history of this region a bold frontiersman made the wrong turn, because of a
maudlin mind acquired in the village by overindulgence in rum, and his wagon,
tipping over, his life was snuffed out on the rocks.

About the year 1870 another devotee of Bacchus became a sacrifice. Before his
team had reached the top of the hill this confused husbandman, thinking he was
at the turn in the road, directed his horses into the rocks and by the overturning of
his wagon-box, was killed.

Another victim was an employee of a hop yard located near the man mound.
One night this individual walked down the slope north of the hill but instead of
following the highway skirting the rocks, he walked directly over the crest. Stepping into the darkness, he fell headlong down the declivity barely escaping death.

Only a few years since, a driver and team came down this same north slope in
a snow storm. The snowdrifts were deep and the driver finally abandoned his con-
veyance, walking behind his horses in an endeavor to follow the road. Blinded by
the falling snow and confused by the drifts, man and team plunged over the cliff
and were only saved from destruction by the abundance of snow. So deep were

the drifts that little could be seen of the horses after the tumble, except their ears.

THE MAN MOUND.

The journey now leads a fraction of a mile farther up the north range of the Baraboo Bluffs, then a mile to the east to Man Mound Park, the central object of which is the famous man mound.

The length of the mound is 214 feet and width at the shoulder 48 feet. In order to assemble this large amount of earth the Indians, having neither shovels nor iron tools of any kind, used bark or other baskets, scrapers of wood or stone, and their hands. The observer will realize with what labor and under what difficulties the workers accomplished their task. When the Indians were gathered here, in camp they, with their activity and fantastic dress, must have presented an unusual picture in the boundless wilderness.

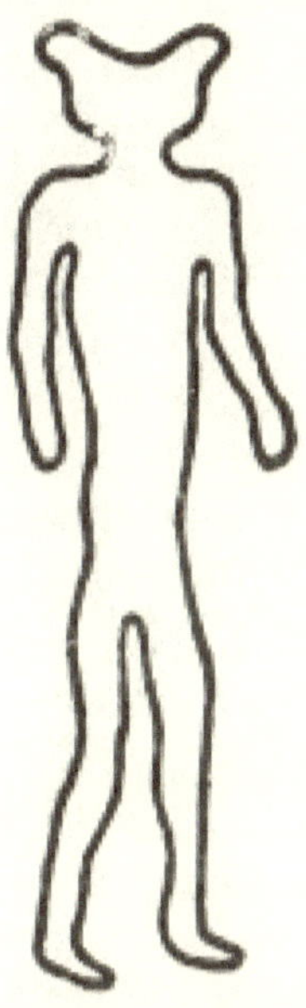

The man mound was located and platted by W. H. Canfield, local surveyor, historian, and archeologist, July 23, 1859. The original survey is now in the possession of the Sauk County Historical Society. The name of the discoverer of this earthwork has been lost in the dimness of time. When the highway was graded a number of years ago the lower part of the legs were destroyed and subsequently the feet, for years beneath a board fence on the north side of the road, were leveled. Why the mound was built is explained near the close of this article.

On August 7, 1908, the Man Mound Park was formally dedicated at a joint state assembly of the Wisconsin Archeological Society and Sauk County Historical Society, the bronze tablet, a gift by J. Van Orden of Baraboo, being unveiled at that time. Previously the land had been purchased by the two societies and the Landmarks Committee of the Wisconsin Federation of Women's Clubs.

REGION RICH IN INDIAN MOUNDS.

In primeval times the Baraboo region was rich in Indian mounds and, although the plow has been active since the 40's and 50's of the last century, many of the aboriginal earthworks still remain. They were erected by the savages on hillside and on plain, by lake, stream, and on the upland, in the deep forest and on the open prairie. They are the relics of a people now disappearing and are of ever increasing interest to the investigating archeologist.

The theory was at one time advanced that a pre-Indian race, the Mound Builders, constructed the earthworks, but modern archeologists have disproved the idea of the existence of any such a pre-historic people, holding the builders of the mounds were none other than the Indians. It is believed the Winnebago are the authors of the majority of the earthworks found in Wisconsin. The great number of these heaps of earth scattered over the country indicate a considerable Indian population extending over no small period of time.

Indian mounds or tumuli are of various forms and, with few exceptions, may be classed as round or conical, elongate or wall-like pyramidal, and effigy or emblematic mounds. The conical mounds in the United States vary in height from scarcely a perceptible swell to elevation of 80 and sometimes 100 feet. Ours are smaller the highest not over 25 feet. Those in the Baraboo region seldom exceed in height of 2, 3, or 4 feet. In the conical mounds the Indians often buried their dead and sometimes one, two, or three layers of charcoal are found above the remains, indicating that fires, probably of a ceremonial nature, had burned over the dead.

The long or wall-like mounds are earthworks of a usual length of 30 to 300 feet, in extreme cases the wall having a maximum extension of 800 or 900 feet. Linear mounds are found in the effigy mound region.

Pyramidal mounds are not found in the Baraboo country.

The effigy mounds represent animal forms, and, with few exceptions, are confined to Wisconsin and contiguous portions of neighboring states. The famous serpent mound and several other animal-shaped earthworks are located in Ohio and two bird mounds are in Georgia. Effigy mounds vary from 3 to 4 to 500 feet in length and in height from a few inches to 5 or 6 feet. Burials were rarely made in these mounds which have the outline of the deer, bear, lizard, turtle, eagle, swallow, frog, or other forms of animal life. Indians are divided into clans and most effigy mounds are believed by archeologists to be the emblems of these. In order to perpetuate the clan idea, the Indians constructed about their places of residence the mounds symbolic of their clans, thousands of these earthen elevations being scattered over southern Wisconsin.

The deer mound at the home of Mrs. Train is a clan emblem but archeologists believe the effigy in Man Mound Park an Indian deity.

Mounds of all types, in the eastern part of Sauk County, numbered over 600, according to a survey made by Dr. A. B. Stout about 1905. Many of the mounds have been leveled by the plow and cultivator.

CHAPTER IX

STONE PILLAR OF CHIEF YELLOW THUNDER

Stone Pillar of Chief Yellow Thunder and His Squaw, Situated a Few
Miles North of Baraboo

Passing the Baraboo Cemetery and continuing for a distance of five miles
north of Baraboo, Yellow Thunder's Pillar is situated where two roads cross. The
stone monument stands but a short distance from where the old chief traversed an
Indian trail and not far from where he died and was buried. On one side appears
the following inscription:

```
*   * * * * * * * * * * * * * * *   *
*        YELLOW THUNDER          *
*       Chief of the Winnebago    *
*       Born 1774—Died 1874       *
*                                 *
*            And His Squaw         *
*               Died 1868          *
*   * * * * * * * * * * * * * * *   *
```

Yellow Thunder, a noted warrior and chief of the Winnebago, was "to the
manor born." With his tribe he probably took part, on the side of the British, in the
War of 1812.

He was buried three days after he had passed to the happy hunting grounds,
his body laid in a box in a horizontal position with face to the west, and his pipe
and various trinkets around. His squaw was interred in similar fashion except that
the body was placed in a sitting position. The ceremonies in both instances were
conducted by Indians, white neighbors assisting only in bearing the bodies to the
graves.

Yellow Thunder is said to have been a "man of great respectability among his
people, and an able councilor in all their public affairs. He was a zealous Catholic."

In an interview, (see Wisconsin Historical Collections) Moses Paquette said of
him that he was a fine looking Indian, tall, straight, and stately, but had an over-
weening love for firewater. This was his only vice.

FORCIBLY REMOVED

YELLOW THUNDER

In 1840 the Indians from this section were forcibly removed by United States troops under the command of Colonel Worth, down the Wisconsin River in boats and canoes to lands west of the Mississippi river. Yellow Thunder and others were invited to Portage to obtain provisions, but instead of that, according to John T. de la Ronde, "were put into the guardhouse, with ball and chain, which hurt the feelings of the Indians very much, as they had done no harm to the government." It is said Yellow Thunder felt the disgrace so keenly he wept. They were afterwards released and taken down the river.

Yellow Thunder, his squaw, and others, however, soon returned, walking some 50 miles and arriving amid familiar scenes before the troops that had taken them away came back. The chief secured forty acres in the town of Fairfield from the government and there he spent much of his time until his death in 1874.

After the demise of his squaw in 1868, Yellow Thunder lived but little in the log house which stood about three-fourths of a mile northeast of the pillar. A few weeks before his death in November, he located his tent on the bank of the Wisconsin river about a mile north of his land in the woods. Here the neighbors ministered to his simple wants, death resulting from an injury to one of his knees, followed by blood poison.

PILLAR ERECTED

In 1909, it was decided by members of the Sauk County Historical Society to remove the remains of Yellow Thunder and his squaw to a new location, fearing that by clearing and cultivating the land the graves would become obliterated. An excavation was made, the bones were placed in a large vitrified tile, and the cairn erected, the earthen receptacle becoming a part of the boulder-made ossuary. Here, near a familiar trail, not far from the white neighbors with whom the Indians often mingled and sometimes ate, the remains rest in this enduring sepulcher.

FROM WAUBUN

The following incidents taken from Wau-Bun, a narrative of the early days at Fort Winnebago, by Mrs. J. H. Kinzie, show some of the characteristics of the squaw of Yellow Thunder.

Among the women with whom I early made acquaintance was the wife of Wau-kaun-zee-kah, the Yellow Thunder. She had accompanied her husband, who was one of the deputation to visit the President, and from that time forth she had been known as "the Washington woman." She had a pleasant, old-acquaintance sort of air in greeting me, as much as to say, "You and I have seen something of the world." No expression of surprise or admiration escaped her lips, as her companions, with childlike laughing simplicity, exclaimed and clapped their hands at the different wonderful objects I showed them. Her deportment said plainly, "Yes, yes, my children, I have seen all these things before." It was not until I put to her ear a tropical shell of which I had a little cabinet, and she heard its murmuring sound, that she laid aside her apathy of manner. She poked her finger into the opening to get at the animal within, shook it violently, then raised it to her ear again, and finally burst into a hearty laugh, and laid it down, acknowledging by her looks, that this was beyond her comprehension.

I had one shell of peculiar beauty—my favorite in the whole collection—a small conch, covered with rich, dark veins. Each of the visitors successively took up this shell, and by words and gestures expressed her admiration, evidently showing that she had an eye for beauty—this was on the occasion of the parting visit of my red daughters.

Shortly after the payment had been completed and the Indians had left, I discovered that my valued shell was missing from the collection. Could it be that one of the squaws had stolen it? It was possible—they would occasionally, though rarely do such things under the influence of strong temptation. I tried to recollect which among the party, looked most likely to have been the culprit. It could not have been the Washington woman—she was partly civilized and knew better.

A few weeks afterward Mrs. Yellow Thunder again made her appearance and carefully unfolding a gay colored chintz shawl, which she carried rolled up in her hand, she produced the shell, and laid it on the table before me. I did not know whether to show by my countenance displeasure at the trick she had played me, or joy at receiving my treasure back again, but at last decided it was the best policy to manifest no emotion whatever.

She prolonged her visit until my husband's return, and he then questioned her about the matter.

"She had taken the shell to her village, to show to some of her people, who did not come to the payment."

"Why had she not asked her mother's leave before carrying it away?"

"Because she saw that her mother liked the shell, and she was afraid she would say, No."

This was not the first instance in which Madame Washington had displayed the shrewdness which was a predominant trait in her character. During the visit of the Indians to the Eastern cities, they were taken to various exhibitions, museums, menageries, theatres, etc. It did not escape their observation that some silver was always paid before entrance and they inquired the reason. It was explained to them. The woman brightened up as if struck with an idea.

"How much do you pay for each one?"

Her father told her.

"How do you say that in English?"

"Two shillings."

"Two shinnin——humph" (good).

The next day, when as usual, visitors began to flock to the rooms where the Indians were sojourning, the woman and a young Indian, her confederate, took their station by the door, which they kept closed. When any one knocked, the door was cautiously opened, and the woman, extending her hand exclaimed—"Two shinnin."

This was readily paid in each instance, and the game went on, until she had accumulated a considerable sum. But this did not satisfy her. At the first attempt of a visitor to leave the room, the door was held close, as before, the hand was extended, and "two shinnin" again met his ear. He tried to explain that, having paid for his entrance, he must go out free. With an innocent shake of the head, "Two shinnin" was all the English she could understand.

The agent, who had entered a short time before, and who overhearing the dialogue, sat laughing behind his newspaper, waiting to see how it would all end, now came forward and interfered, and the guests were permitted to go forth without further contribution.

CHAPTER X

PORTAGE AND FORT WINNEBAGO

Portage and Old Fort Winnebago—Cemetery Where Soldiers of Several Wars Are Buried—Waubun House

When Wisconsin was on the frontier, as a protection against the Indians, three forts were built—Fort Howard at Green Bay, Fort Crawford at Prairie du Chien, and Fort Winnebago at Portage. The central object of interest in this little journey is the early outpost at the Fox-Wisconsin portage.

Leaving Baraboo on Trunk Line 33, leading directly east of the city, where open fields now greet the eye on either side, was once a treeless tract known as Peck's Prairie. This was named for Eben Peck, an early settler whose residence was on the present highway a short distance west of the fair ground.

ROCHE MOUTONNEE

After passing a road which turns to the left and leads to the man mound, a roche moutonnee, sheep shaped surface of the quartzite, may be seen about a half-mile to the left. The surface of the outcrop was rounded during the invasion of the glacial ice into this region.

Just before reaching the Baraboo River the road swings to the left, approaching the talused slope of the rugged north range of the Baraboo Bluffs. Two species of cacti grow on the summit here, also to the west—Opuntia humifusa, the western prickly pear, and Opuntia fragilis, the brittle opuntia.

The road runs on the verge of a dry ravine, where an Indian effigy mound reposes on the opposite bank, near the Baraboo River. Other mounds were to the west and an Indian ford crossed the stream here. About 1906 an Indian skeleton was unearthed on the bank of the gully, nearly opposite the farmstead.

GARRISONVILLE

In the region about the ravine, Mrs. Ann Garrison, in pioneer times, laid out a paper city, much to the regret of lot purchasers in Philadelphia and elsewhere. The sawmill, the pottery, the hotel, and the "salted" gold mine are but memories now.

The gap where the river escapes from the valley into the lowland to the north, has a geological history similar to that of Devil's Lake. No talus covers the slopes, however, the loose stones having been swept away when the ice sheet flowed slowly through in glacial times.

AN ANCIENT LAVA BED

At seven localities about the outer margin of the quartzite region, igneous rocks have been found—at Alloa, near the Devil's Nose, at Baxter's Hollow, three near Denzer and the Lower Narrows.

By far the largest area, fully described by Professor Samuel Weidman in "The Baraboo Iron-Bearing District," is found at the Lower Narrows, distributed over the width of more than half a mile along the north slope, to the east and west of the gap. At the bridge the road to the left leads to a point less than a mile distant, here the igneous rock or rhyolite comes boldly within a few feet of the highway. By climbing upon the ledge one stands on a surface older than the Baraboo Hills, older than any deposit in the whole region. As lava the rhyolite flowed, then cooled and during the upheaval of the north range was forced upon its edge, remaining so to this day. Upon this cooled lava the whole later geologic formation of the region rests—to be upon it is to be upon the floor of the world.

JEFFERSON DAVIS

FORT WINNEBAGO IN 1834

ROAD HUGS THE BLUFF

Eastward from the bridge over the Baraboo River, the highway hugs the bluff. A few Indian mounds may be seen less than half a mile to the north after passing the first farm house. To the east of these mounds the skeletons of about sixty Indians were uncovered when one was leveled a number of years ago. The Indian corpses had been seated in a circle and buried in one heap of earth. Evidently there had been a battle or pestilence amongst them.

Reduced facsimile of oil painting by Ira A. Ridgeway of Portage in 1896, based on contemporary plans and recollections of early settlers. The view is from the southwest. The building to the right of the gate is the guardhouse; to the left, the armory. On the opposite side of the square, to the left, were the officers' quarters. The peakedroof building at the left corner was a blockhouse, and a similar structure was in the corner diagonally opposite. The magazine appears in the corner adjacent to the guardhouse, and at its side to the right were soldiers' quarters. The chapel was in the corner diagonally opposite the magazine, but is not visible; as is the case with some of the other smaller buildings. The log building near the end of the bridge over the Fox river, to the right, was Henry Merrell's sutler's store. The low structure a little to the east was the ice cellar. A little further along was the surgeon's headquarters and to the right the hospital. In the distance, looking between the hospital and surgeon's quarters, may be seen the old stone bakery; the blacksmith shop and the carpenter shop were close by, but do not appear in the picture. At the left of the bridge is a commissary building; just to its rear was Jones's store, a portion is discernible. Beyond the fort to the left (out of the above picture) was a log theatre. Still further to the left, was the Indian Agency building. An enormous well was in the exact center of the stockade. It is in use at the present time.

To the right of the highway are many hidden beauty spots all along the way to the Baraboo River, especially where the streams come down from the high land above. The most attractive of these is Fox's Glen, to the right and just east of the rural school building facing the river.

The high ground on the right, just before crossing the bridge over the Wisconsin River, is the site of an Indian village. The pioneers crossed the river here on a ferry, the first bridge being built in 1857. It was destroyed by a cyclone in 1903, and the present structure was then erected.

HOME OF AN AUTHOR

After entering West Cook Street, the main thoroughfare of Portage, and reaching the third street to the right, the car should be swung one block south to pass the home of Miss Zona Gale. The residence, 506 West Canal Street, is southern colonial in architecture, and stands on the bank of the winding Wisconsin, the rear lawn sloping back to the waterway.

SCENE OF A DARK DEED

One block to the left and one block to the north, brings the visitor to the intersection of West Cook and Mac Streets; here Pierre Pauquette, the Indian trader, interpreter, and portager was killed by an aborigine. The deed was committed, it is said, a little southwest of the intersection of the streets.

Pauquette was one of the most picturesque figures in the early days of Wisconsin, indissolubly identified with those who cast their lot at the portage.

MONUMENT TO DISCOVERERS

Crossing the canal bridge near the Wisconsin River and continuing south several blocks, a granite monument marks the place where Jacques Marquette and Louis Joliet, the first white men to visit this region, crossed the portage on June 14, 1673, and floated down the Wisconsin.

Many noted persons crossed the portage in early times. Duluth and Hennepin were here in 1680 and Nicolas Perrot, the Baron Lahontan, and Charles Pierre Le Sueur were three famous travelers in the late seventeenth century. An expedition to build a French fort on the upper Mississippi, passed here in 1727; Johnathan Carver tells of his visit in 1766; and here was the rendezvous for Indian forces during the American Revolution. An expedition against St. Louis gathered here in 1780. Then came the much passing of troops between Fort Howard at Green Bay and Fort Crawford at Prairie du Chien. Here in 1827 occurred the dramatic surrender of Red Bird, bringing to a close the Winnebago War.

In 1793 Laurent Barth came to transport baggage with oxen, in 1801-2 Augustin Grignon wintered at the portage as a fur trader, and in 1810 the overland division of the Astorian expedition to the Pacific coast went westward over this historic route.

During the war of 1812 Robert Dixon, British Indian agent, collected his savage allies at this point; and the expedition which drove the Americans from Prairie du Chien, passed thither in 1814. By this route the British forces, following the treaty of Ghent, retreated in 1815.

AN EARLY HOSTELRY

Carpenter's place was on the corner to the south of the monument. In a building near the pioneer hotel, Abe Wood killed Pawnee Blanc, buried in a mound near the Portage-end of the Wisconsin River bridge.

Continuing on Bronson Avenue to the east and after crossing the railroad tracks, the location of the Franklin House may be seen several rods to the right. A large elm tree with a small house back of it marks the location of the pioneer Portage hotel where dignitaries of the early days were entertained.

The Riverbend Place, the home of Mr. and Mrs. A. J. Stace, is the last house before crossing the Fox River. To the rear of this house is where Henry Merrill, the sutler of Fort Winnebago, resided.

FORT WINNEBAGO

After crossing the stream, the location of the commissary building of the fort will be observed a few rods to the left. Goods from boats plying the Fox were unloaded into the building; a fragment of the wall still remains, hidden in the weeds and grass.

The frame house to the right, somewhat modified, was the fort hospital.

The well at the farmstead at the left was in the center of Fort Winnebago when completed in 1830. The portage was made a military post in 1828, Major David E. Twiggs erecting the fortification. During the Black Hawk War the outpost was useful in checking the hostile tribesmen, it remained a garrison until 1845, and was sold in 1853, the nineteen and fifteen-hundredths acres bringing $23.94. The old deed is in the Portage Library.

Colonel Zachary Taylor, afterward president of the United States, visited the fort with Captain Hugh Brady, Indian fighter, in 1836, and Lieutenant Jefferson Davis, later president of the confederacy, came with the military force to construct and garrison the place. Judge D. Doty, afterward territorial governor, often was there, while General Lewis Cass, and Captain Frederick Marryat, celebrated English novelist, were among the many noted visitors. Miss Marcy, later the wife of General George B. McClellan, was a child here, the daughter of a lieutenant.

THE OLD CEMETERY

Continuing on the central of the three roads about a quarter of a mile, the Fort Winnebago cemetery will be found in a grove to the right. Near the west fence is the grave of Cooper Pixley, a soldier of the Revolution, who died in 1855, aged 86.

A little to the east is the grave of William Sylvester, a soldier of the War of 1812, and the first mayor of Portage. He was born October 28, 1792, and died November 20, 1875. His two wives sleep beside him.

Near the center of the cemetery is the grave of Henry Carpenter, a soldier in the Black Hawk War, and hard by are the graves of Civil War veterans, while the body of Archie White Eagle, a Winnebago Indian veteran of the World War, also sleeps in the enclosure.

Those who died in the fort are buried along the south fence. The boards marking their graves burned years ago and their locations are now lost.

Some of the graves in the cemetery are those who came to the lead region in early times and later to the portage.

Returning toward Portage, cross the canal at the eastern extremity of the city, turn sharply to the right and follow the road on the bank of the artificial waterway to the Agency or Waubun House, now owned by Attorney E. S. Baker. John H. Kinzie came with his bride to the portage in 1830 and this house was soon after erected for them. Mrs. Kinzie brought her piano up the Fox River in a boat, mention of which is made in her delightful Wau-Bun.

Near the Agency House Four Legs, chief of the Winnebago, was buried.

The lock where the canal joins the Fox is a short distance to the east of the historic house, and the blacksmith shop was in the field forty rods or more to the west.

BURIAL PLACE OF PAUQUETTE

Returning along the canal, crossing the railroad, and traversing East Cook street near the center of the city, a turn is made to the right at the Baptist Church. Between the church and the parsonage to the rear stood the first French Mission between Depere and Prairie du Chien, erected with logs by Pierre Pauquette in 1833-34. He was killed by an Indian in 1836 and beneath the rude place of worship was buried. According to a tablet on the parsonage, the remains of Pauquette were exhumed in 1904. They now repose in the Catholic cemetery.

CHAPTER XI

BOYHOOD HOMES OF JOHN MUIR

Boyhood Haunts of John Muir, the Naturalist—Fountain Lake—Father a Disciple—the Muir Family

Before making this journey, by all means read "My Boyhood and Youth," by John Muir, naturalist and author, a cherished volume in public libraries. To visit an historic spot or home of a famous character without familiarizing oneself with the associations and incidents that make the place of interest, is to lose the keenest enjoyment. What we fully appreciate, affords the greatest delight. Therefore, before seeking the lake and farm homes once dear to the heart of this Scotch boy of rare endowments, the mind should be fresh with the details of his early struggles and attainments as well as those of his later years.

FROM BARABOO

Trunk Line 33 takes one from Baraboo to Portage and after leaving the eastern extremity of the main street in the latter city, the highway winds over the Fox River, then up a slight incline to where three roads meet. The one to the left, known as the Montello road, leads to the earliest Muir home. The historic Fox River is often visible from the highway. Arriving at the first school building, where Annie and Joanna Muir, sisters of the naturalist, taught, the road makes a turn to the right a quarter of a mile, then deflects to the left to another school located on the right where the Muir children were given instruction after their arrival in Wisconsin from Scotland in 1849. Neither of the school buildings is that actually familiar to the Muirs as the early structures have long since yielded to the ravages of time.

Just beyond the last named school, some ten miles from Portage, a little stream murmurs across the highway and a few rods farther on is a weather-beaten farm house. The stream flows from Ennis or Fountain Lake to the Fox River and the simple dwelling is near the site of the first home of the Muirs after their emigration to the western wilderness.

The old frame house, with its curious hand-carved frieze boards at the gable ends of the roof, is not the original home of the Muirs, their pioneer abode being located to the rear of the present domicile. It was a little farther from the highway and long since destroyed by fire.

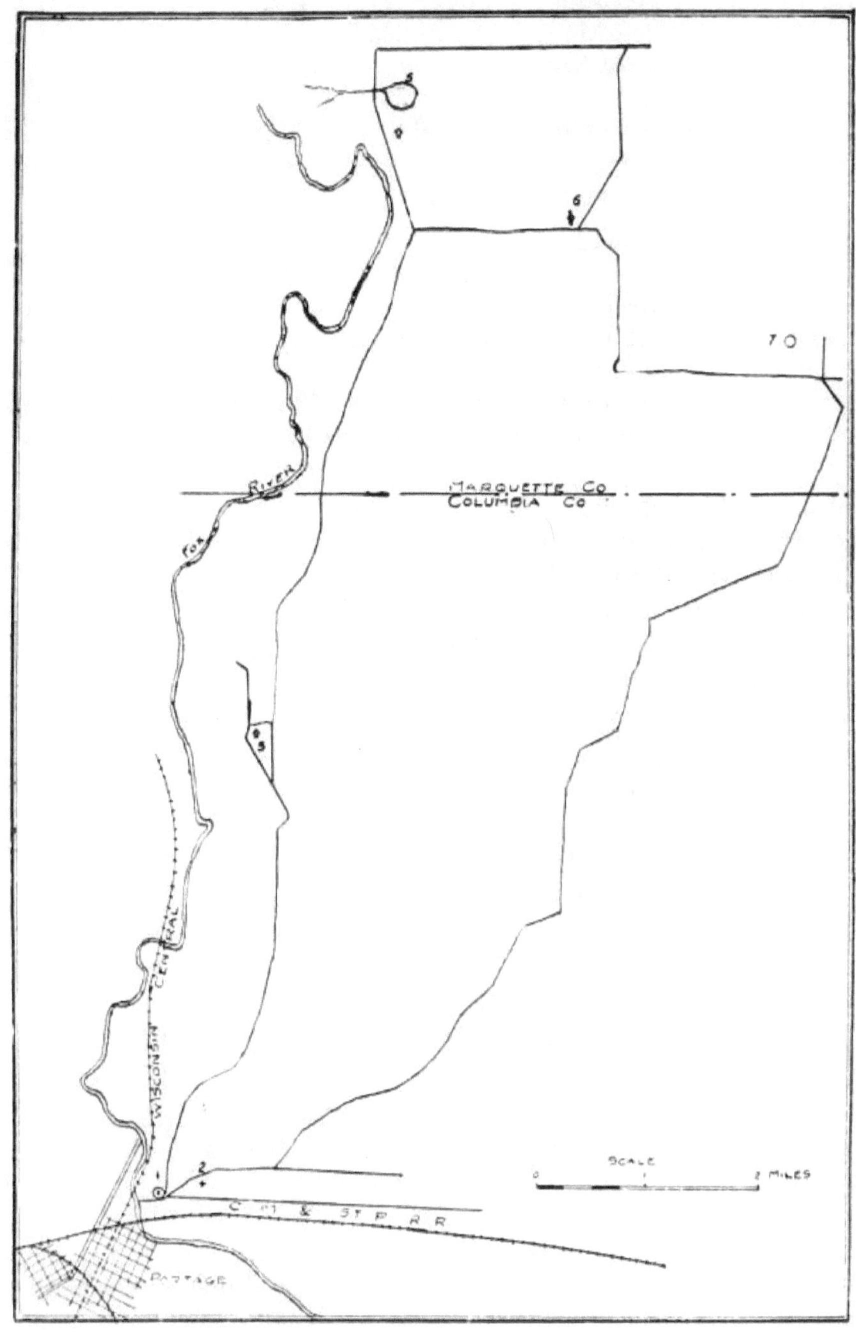

LITTLE JOURNEY TO HOMES OF JOHN MUIR

(1) Fort Winnebago
(2) Fort Winnebago Cemetery

(3) School Where Annie and Johanna Muir Taught
(4) School Where Muir Children Attended
(5) Fountain Lake, first home of Muir family.
(6) Muir church.
(7) Second home of the Muir family.

THE LAKE

But the lake still shimmers in the sun as of old. No ridge of rock encroaches on its shores, which are low and lush with grasses, ferns and other vegetation. Over this water John Muir rowed, in it he swam, and on one occasion nearly lost his life, as related in the story of his youthful days. The diversions which the lake afforded were never ending. Muir speaking of it says: "The water was so clear that it was almost invisible, and when we floated slowly out over the plants and fishes, we seemed to be miraculously sustained in the air while silently exploring a veritable fairyland."

Bluejays, kingbirds, blackbirds, buntings, kingfishers and other descendants of the feathered comrades of John Muir and his brothers, still inhabit its shores, delighting the visitor as they flit from tree to tree.

Ennis Lake is the name given on the government topographical maps to this sheet of water but it was known as Fountain Lake when the Muirs resided there. It should bear the name of Muir.

This Muir farm is now owned by James McReath, son of the Mr. McReath (spelled McRath in the book) mentioned by Muir. The present owner of the old homestead knew the Muir family and will tell the visitor interesting things about the household. Here it was the pet coon fished in the sparkling stream and was called "my little man" by the Highland Scotchman. He would say:

"Coonie, ma mannie, Coonie, ma mannie, how are ye the day? I think you're hungry," as the comical pet began to examine his pockets for nuts and bread,— "Na, na there's na-thing in my pocket for ye the day, my wee mannie, but I'll get ye something."

The McReaths came to Wisconsin in 1850, the year following the Muirs.

FATHER A DISCIPLE

The father of John Muir was of a religious mind, an earnest student of the Bible. He was a member of the Disciple or Christian Church and often held services in the Fountain Lake home.

Returning toward Portage about one mile from the site of the first Muir home, then going about as far to the east over a sandy road, one observes a church standing near the tombs in the churchyard. Here it was that the senior Muir conducted service, no doubt pronouncing the last rites for some of those who sleep there. The gravestones are marked with many names familiar to Scotts, among them are Mair, Owen, Thompson, Graham and McDougal.

Turning to the right almost a mile, then to the left a slightly greater distance, brings one to Hickory Hill Farm, the second Muir home. The house is located some distance from the highway and may be approached through the farm, either from the south or east. The farm is not as sandy as the one near the Fox River and when the Muirs came to this location the father purchased five 80's and a 40 in one tract. The family occupied the land for many years. While residing here, John Muir arranged numerous clever contrivances on gates and doors about the farm and buildings, but none of these remained when, long after he had become a famous naturalist, he visited the farm about 1898. The house, with some changes, still stands; the cellar into which John retreated to study and work remains; the well in which he almost lost his life yields abundant water; and some of the apple trees planted by the Muirs rejoice the present owners with juicy fruit each returning autumn. The barn has been elevated and moved but the old timbers familiar to the Muir family have withstood the storms of many seasons. Much of the land on this farm was plowed for the first time by the naturalist and from this home he went to the University of Wisconsin, loaded with curious contraptions, to realize after a sojourn there a new world of natural wonders.

This farm was sold to John C. McHaffy when the Muirs moved to Portage and after two years passed to Thomas Kearns, the present owner, who talks entertainingly of the famous family.

THE MUIR FAMILY

Father—Daniel Muir, born in England in 1802 or 1803 (date is not certain), and died in Kansas City, Mo., 1883.

Mother—Mrs. Daniel Muir, nee Anne Gilrye, born in Dunbar, Scotland, March 17, 1813; married Daniel Muir, 1833. They were married in Dunbar, Scotland, and there John Muir was born. Mrs. Muir died in Portage, Wis., June, 1896.

The Children—

Margaret, born September, 1834; married John Reid, December 1860; died at Martinez, California, June, 1910.

Sarah, born February 19, 1836; married David M. Galloway, December, 1856; lives in Pacific Grove, California.

John, born April 21, 1838; died in Los Angeles, California, December 24, 1914; buried near Martinez, California.

David Gilrye, born July 11, 1840; died at Pacific Grove, California, October 28, 1916; buried at Martinez, California.

Daniel Muir, born June 29, 1843; lives in Lincoln, Nebraska.

Mary and Annie, twins, born October 5, 1846; Mary married Willis Hand; her home is at Kearney, Nebraska; Annie died January 15, 1903, at Portage, Wisconsin, seven years after the demise of her mother.

Joanna Gilrye, born on September 7, 1850; married L. Walter Brown September 1, 1880; lives in Ivyland, Pennsylvania.

Angling is the road from this farm to Portage, a distance of some ten miles.

CHAPTER XII

WISCONSIN HEIGHTS BATTLEFIELD—NATURAL BRIDGE

Wisconsin Heights Battlefield—About a Mile From Sauk City—Another Napoleon Soldier Grave

The memorable battle of Wisconsin Heights, between U. S. troops and the famous Indian chief, Black Hawk, and his Sac and Fox warriors, was fought about a mile southwest of Sauk City. This encounter, so disastrous to the forces of Black Hawk, took place June 21, 1832, when Wisconsin still was a part of Michigan territory and settlements were chiefly in the lead region, now the southwestern section of the state.

The major portion of the journey to this historic battlefield is over Trunk Line No. 12, which climbs the terminal moraine two miles southwest of Baraboo, traverses an outwash plain, crosses Skillet Creek, rounding the point recorded by geologists as the mouth of an ancient stream as shown by successive layers of fluvial deposit, and skirting a bold outcrop of quartzite, ascends the range to the summit of the bluff. From the elevated highway one obtains a charming view of beautiful Sauk Prairie where, year after year, the horn of Amalthaea is most prodigal with gifts. This outwash plain was a veritable paradise of bloom in the days before the advent of the plow.

A PAPER TOWN

At the bottom of the bluff, between the first and second roads which course to the right, lies the village plat of New Haven. The surveyor's map of this "paper" town is preserved in the courthouse in Baraboo.

The last mile of the road leading into Prairie du Sac follows one of the oldest highways in the county. It was part of a stage line to Baraboo in an early day and the progenitor of the present scenic system of roads among the Baraboo hills.

Just above the villages of Prairie du Sac and Sauk City, the Wisconsin River has been harnessed and many thousand horse-power from the great dam provides light and force for an extensive area.

From Prairie du Sac the road leads along the river a mile into Sauk City. The villages have been rivals since they came into existence in the early 40's, when they were the first centers of population north and west of the river in this section of the state. Many of the dwellings in Sauk City follow a fashion in architecture common in central Europe but rarely seen in this country.

APPROACHING THE HEIGHTS

Crossing the Wisconsin River at Sauk City, turning to the right and following the Mazomanie highway about one mile, a crossroad is reached beyond which is a small stream spanned by a bridge. Ahead of this bridge and to the left looms Wisconsin Heights, a rugged elevation from which the battle between the forces of General Dodge and Black Hawk and his warriors takes its name.

CAUSES OF THE BATTLE

The causes leading up to the battle of Wisconsin Heights were numerous. On the Rock River, near its confluence with the Mississippi was the Sac village, the inhabitants of which were more in sympathy with the British than the Americans at that time. Treaties had been signed by the Indians transferring to the whites their common lands but when the time came for them to give up their holdings, the red men declared their chiefs had not authority to sign away the territory and refused to leave. As early as 1823 white squatters enraged Chief Black Hawk and his people by burning their lodges, destroying their crops, and insulting their squaws, while the chief and his braves were absent on the hunt. Black Hawk was advised to seek a village site beyond the Mississippi to avoid the advancing tide of settlement but the warrior was obstinate and prepared to fight for his lands. A crisis was reached in 1830 when pioneers plowed over an Indian cemetery, preempted a village site, and took possession of the planting grounds of the red men. Black Hawk, after consulting with the British agent, threatened the squatters with force, but a military demonstration so frightened the Indians that they gave up the idea of fighting and fled across the Mississippi.

WAR BEGINS

On April 6, 1832, the Hawk, with about five hundred warriors, mostly Sac Indians, crossed into Illinois, creating wild excitement in the settlements there and in Wisconsin. Soon eighteen hundred volunteers, some mounted and some on foot, were on the march. Black Hawk sent a note of defiance, retreated up the Rock River, and made a stand at Stillman's Creek. Disappointed in not receiving assistance from other tribes, he sent messengers with a white flag to his pursuers, asking that he might return peaceably beyond the Mississippi. Those bearing the white flag were brutally slain by the militia, Black Hawk was enraged, and from an ambush routed a larger party, killing a number and wounding others.

About this time settlers were killed at a number of places and the name of Black Hawk was connected with every stump, tree, and projecting rock in the region. The entire section was terrified. Forts sprang up at a dozen place and additional troops were summoned.

In the meantime Black Hawk moved up Rock River to near Lake Koshkonong and, being hotly pursued, retreated with his warriors and the women and children to the present site of the city of Madison.

A DAY OF EXCITEMENT

The Indians and the militia were on the move early on the morning of July 21, 1832. Their camps had been near each other but neither cared to make an attack at night. While passing along the shore of one of the lakes at Madison, an Indian was seen to come up from the water and pause near a newly made grave. In a moment he was pierced with bullets. The grave was probably that of his squaw who had died from exhaustion and the disconsolate red man had decided to await the approaching foe and there, also, meet his fate.

It was not long until the rear of the band was sighted. The day was warm. The Indians threw away kettles, blankets and other weighty articles in order to accelerate their speed. Some forty horses belonging to the soldiers became exhausted, and the riders leaped from the animals and hurried along as fast as possible on foot. Two or three times the Indians showed fight but melted away as soon as any number of their enemies appeared. These feints but served to spur the militia forward. The pursuit was ruthless, exciting, and determined, a chase from dawn to late afternoon.

Black Hawk did not have over 500 warriors, while General Henry had about 600 soldiers and Colonel Dodge 150 more. In the ardour of their pursuit, over a country possessing many difficulties, the immediate commands of Colonel Dodge and Colonel Ewing had outstripped the rest of General Henry's brigade. About five o'clock in the afternoon, when they arrived at Wisconsin Heights, they were met by a spy company which had preceded them and which had been driven back, the enemy having shown fight. The command of Dodge, with Ewing in the center, dismounted, formed in line, and advanced to the edge of the bluff. The Indians were secreted in the high grass growing on the level ground on both sides of the stream. Dodge maintained his position for about an hour; General Henry's brigade then arriving. His soldiers were deployed to the right and left, the line thus being formed with Dodge's command in the center.

From five o'clock until sundown the conflict continued. The Indians in the meantime had been driven from their initial position, some of them escaping up the bank south of the stream and others falling back in the rank verdure toward the Wisconsin. Rain fell and the high grass becoming wet, it was found impossible for the men to keep their arms dry in passing through it, so the firing ceased.

ALLIES OF THE WHITES

Chief White Crow, father of Yellow Thunder's squaw, buried a few miles north of Baraboo, a number of Winnebago, and Pierre Pauquette, their interpreter, were in the battle as aids to the whites. They had joined a detachment which had left Fort Winnebago (Portage) to go to Rock River, and were in the wild chase across the unbroken country to the place of the battle. They left the scene during the night and returned to Fort Winnebago.

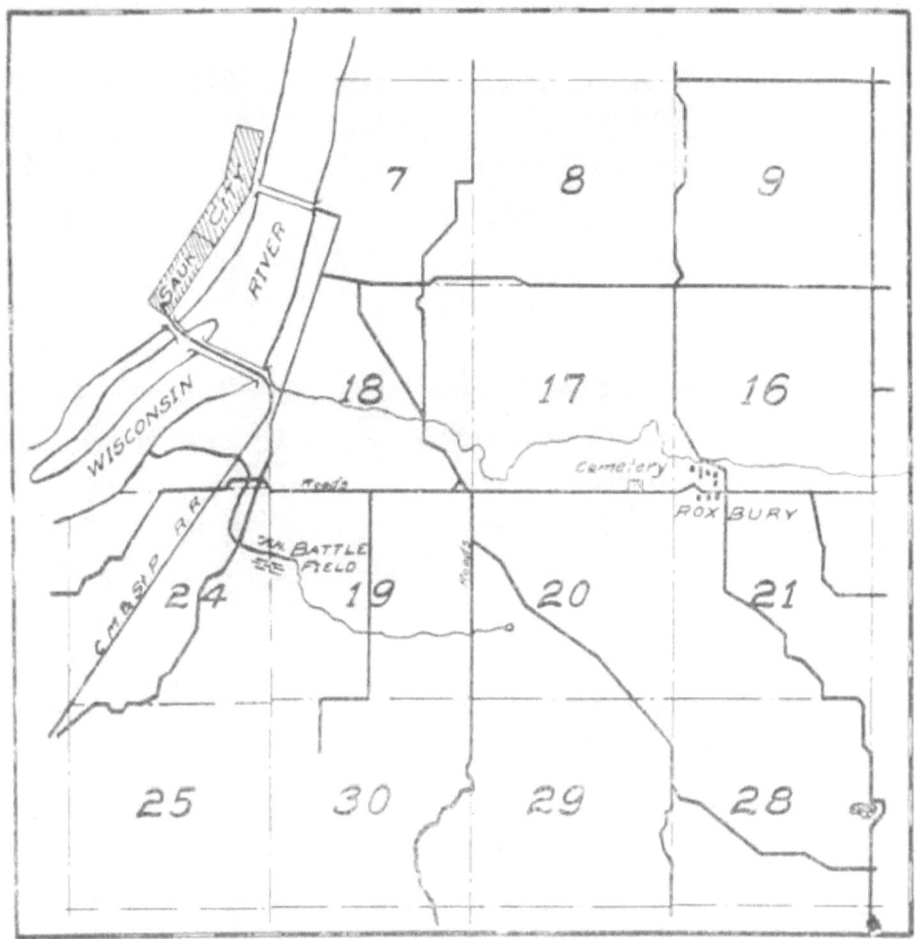

WISCONSIN HEIGHTS BATTLEFIELD

On the mountain overlooking the battlefield, an Indian chief gave orders during the fight and a little before dawn the morning after, a voice was heard from the same eminence. This greatly disturbed the troops and General Henry had all of his men parade in order of battle. The individual speaking in the darkness was Neapope, endeavoring to make a conciliation, thinking the Winnebago were still in the camp and would understand him. Just before daylight the harangue ceased and Neapope disappeared. When morning came troops found a few horse tracks which appeared to have been made during the night.

AN UNMARKED GRAVE

But one soldier was killed, John Short, who is buried on the bank among the trees, a few rods south of the stream and east of the highway. All trace of his grave is lost. A young woman, Mary Hackett, who died in pioneer times, was buried at the eastern extremity of the level ground, not far from where the soldier was interred. No one has since been buried here.

NATURAL BRIDGE NEAR LELAND

During the battle Colonel Jones had a horse shot from under him and several soldiers were wounded. The day after the fight was spent in preparing to transfer the injured to the fort at Blue Mounds.

The number of Indians killed will never be known, but was in the neighborhood of fifty or sixty. Many of the survivors, with hearts of lead, crossed the Wisconsin River during the night, and moved through the wilderness in a northwesternly direction toward the Mississippi.

In his autobiography, Black Hawk says that "Whatever may be the sentiments of the white people in relation to this battle, my nation, though fallen, will award to me the reputation of a great brave in conducting it." Evidently he was proud of his conduct in this particular fight.

JEFFERSON DAVIS IN THE BATTLE

Jefferson Davis, later president of the Southern Confederacy, likewise participated in the Battle of Wisconsin Heights. After he had fought with distinction in the Mexican war, and had served as secretary of war in President Pierce's cabinet, and after holding the position of commander-in-chief of the southern armies for four years during the Civil War, he supported Black Hawk's claim to the military skill he had displayed in this battle. Davis speaks of the tactics employed by the chief as the most brilliant he had ever witnessed, saying: "Had it been performed by white men, it would have been immortalized as one of the most splendid achievements in military history."

INDIANS PURSUED

A few days after the battle, troops crossed the Wisconsin at Arena, marched up the bank of the river until the trail was found, and pursued the retreating Indians. The savages killed horses along the way in order to sustain themselves with food; some perished from their wounds, and still others died from fatigue. At the mouth of the Bad Axe River, the troops from the rear, the fire from the Warrior on the Mississippi, and the Indians in Minnesota, almost annihilated the band of the deluded, deceived, and defeated Black Hawk. A few of his braves and families who descended the Wisconsin river in boats, met a similar fate near the mouth of the stream, bringing to an end the cons'n.

A. L. Taylor resides on a farm a short distance east of the battlefield. When a youth he accompanied a soldier who fought in the battle, also his father, over the ground. Mr. Taylor has a clear recollection of the description of the fight given by the participant in the battle. Years ago Mr. Taylor's father found on the field a gun and saddle, afterwards destroyed in a farmhouse fire.

A short distance south of where John Short is buried there is a fine group of Indian mounds.

GRAVE OF A NAPOLEON SOLDIER

From the Mazomanie road near the battlefield, one may drive east about a mile to the Roxbury Cemetery, on Trunk Line 12. Near the center of this Catholic burying ground lies a soldier who served one year against Napoleon and three years under him, a not uncommon circumstance when the whole of Europe was torn by the great Corsican. The inscription above the grave reads:

```
*  * * * * * * * * * * * * * * * * * * * * * * * * *  *
*              Peter Pauli                *
*           Geb. 10, June, 1792           *
*           Gest. 7, Sept., 1884          *
*                 R. I. P.                *
*        Schlafe Wohl, O Vater Schlafe    *
*          Deiner Walfahrt Leiden aus     *
*   Sanft Sei Dir Der Letzte Schlummer    *
*        Dein Erwachen Ohne Kummer        *
*  * * * * * * * * * * * * * * * * * * * * * * * * *  *
```

About 1848 Pauli came with his family to America and after a stay in Milwaukee settled in Roxbury, where he died. It is said there are two other Napoleon soldiers buried in this cemetery but their graves have not been identified.

Within site of the cemetery is the Roxbury church, one of the richest rural churches in this section of the state and one which dates to territorial times.

On the return after passing over the bridge at Sauk City, the street due west crosses the railroad track and but a short distance beyond in an oak grove to the left, may be seen about an acre of Indian corn hills. Much of the ground at Prairie du Sac and Sauk City was devoted by the Indians to the growing of vegetables. These corn hills among the oaks are the only ones remaining, now sward covered and much reduced in elevation.

On the knoll or ridge, north of the highway and near the railroad, may be seen some old buildings among a few trees. Here in the spring of 1854, Professor H. J. Turner opened a French and English boarding school, which supplied educational facilities to the community for several years.

NATURAL BRIDGE

From Prairie du Sac there is a paved road all the way to Leland, a distance of some fifteen miles. About a mile east of the last named village may be seen the Natural Bridge. Passing the third house east of the church the car should be stopped where the road bends a little to the left, beyond sight of a farm house and almost in view of the church steeple in the village. In the edge of the wood, several rods north of the road, the natural bridge may be seen. This massive and unusual curiosity, eroded from the sandstone, is on land owned by Richard Radatz.

The return to Baraboo may be made by continuing to the east through Denzer, joining Trunk Line 12 near Kings Corners.

CHAPTER XIII

PARFREY'S GLEN

Parfrey's Glen, Wildest of Them All, a Cool Retreat, Prodigal in Charm—Mill a Memory

Parfrey's Glen is a rugged gash in the south range of the Baraboo Bluffs. This ravine, an interesting objective for tourists, is about a mile down the slope from Wawanissee Point and some five or six miles east of Devil's Lake. It derives its name from Robert Parfrey, an early resident.

The little stream which has cut this wildly beautiful glen had a romantic history of usefulness in early days. At the present time it is secondary in interest to the Glen itself, the first glimpse of which enthralls the visitor, urging him to journey to the end.

The route from Baraboo to Parfrey's is along the Merrimack road in a southeasterly direction. It leads up a bluff, then down on the opposite side, turning to the left and clinging close to the base of the elevation for some two miles, until it turns into the farmstead of August Roese, located a quarter of a mile north of the main highway. Here the car is abandoned. To reach the Glen a tramp of a half mile is necessary, along a trail which leads over glacial boulders, across a mountain stream, and up a winding way to the opening. The view, as one progresses, includes a charming expanse of rich countryside.

WILDEST OF THEM ALL

Compared with the other glens of the region, Parfrey's is by far the wildest. The south wall of this ancient cleft in the bluff is almost perpendicular. Only occasionally does an overhanging ledge afford a footing for wood creature or habitation for shrub or fern. High above pines, birches, oaks and other small timber crowd the brink. The cut shows a mass of sandstone and quartzite conglomerate which have been exposed through a long period of erosion. The north slope is clothed in green. Rugged rocks lie along the purling stream, as if cast there by giant hands to impede the pathway. Between them flourish ferns, mosses and an interesting number of native plants. Looking down from the top of the opening the water winds in and out among the moss-clad stones like a translucent ribbon, making soft music whose melody is lost as the stream finds its way to the grass-land. Many birds haunt the Glen; the indigo bunting, the oriole, and scarlet tanager with their brilliant coloring contrast sharply with the grey of the rocks. The note of the song sparrow, the trill of the thrush, and the less marked twitter of many other varieties are heard with delightful frequency.

This cool retreat, so prodigal in charm and comparatively easy of access, should be more widely known than it is to visitors to the Baraboo region.

MILL, A MEMORY

In early days the Glen-stream was harnessed to a sawmill located near the ravine. Evidences of the ancient, earthen dam are visible to this day. In later years a gristmill made use of the power, for some time serving the surrounding community. A story which illustrates the extent of these activities, particularly that of the gristmill, is often related. It seems that the miller was one day greatly puzzled at the non-appearance of flour as his wheels ground round and round. Searching for the cause, it is said, he finally came upon an intruder, no other than a small grey mouse, which was devouring the product of his mill as fast as it sifted through. Also it is told that a distillery at one time, by the aid of the little stream, converted corn from the neighboring fields into "robin hop." During this interval the Glen seemed in grave danger of becoming a popular resort for all those who suffered with a barleycorn thirst and a desire for seclusion. Fortunately for the reputation of the locality, the existence of the worm in the wilderness was brief.

Save for the turf-covered ruins of the ancient dam, all record of the early enterprises is obliterated and memories of the Glen's activities alone remain.

CHAPTER XIV

DURWARD'S GLEN

Durward's Glen—Short History of the Durward Family—Attractive
Features of Interesting Place

From Baraboo to Durward's Glen is a trip of exceptional interest and scenic beauty. The ten-mile drive over a picturesque highway which stretches along the backbone of the south range of the Baraboo Bluffs affords rare glimpses of open valleys and wooded slopes, with the Wisconsin River visible in the distance. The Glen, the erstwhile home of the gifted Durward family, is a delightful retreat where the visitor is welcome to spread his lunch by the murmuring trout stream, enjoy the natural beauty of the spot, and the charm of interesting association.

WAY TO THE GLEN

In journeying to the Glen, variety of view is obtained by taking the road, from Baraboo, on top of the bluffs and returning by the main highway. The Merrimack road leads via Ringlingville, through Glenville, and on up the bluff to the flat top about three miles from town. Following the first turn to the left a level tract is soon noticed on the right as the machine passes a German Lutheran church and public school. On the unbroken surface reposed a glacial lake hemmed in on one side by ice, and on the other by the hills. But a short distance beyond, on the left, kettle holes (cavities left by melting blocks of ice) may be seen, also the terminal moraine, a ridge of land but a few rods away.

POINT SAUK

About two miles from the church, where the road curves slightly to the right, a by-road disappears between a farmhouse and barn, formerly the P. Fitzsimmons homestead. Less than a quarter of a mile from the main road, to the right as one proceeds, is Point Sauk, the most elevated land in the entire region, 1620 feet high. Here one obtains an extensive view. With a glass the capitol dome at Madison, 285 feet high, the highest but one in the United States and the highest but three in the world, nearly thirty miles away, may be seen on the horizon.

Continuing on the main road less than a half-mile to Wawanissee Point. Lake Wisconsin may be seen in the hazy distance, the village of Merrimack being hidden on the right.

Stepping into the wooded pasture and ascending a knoll, a wonderous view is enjoyed. The checkered farms, the shimmering lake, the distant hills combine in making one of the charming pictures of the region. Wawanissee is an Indian word which means beauty or beautiful.

FOUNTAIN AT DURWARD'S GLEN

To the left, this side of the river, the Owl's Head, a knot of an elevation, lifts itself above the surrounding country.

Turning to the left at the T in the road, swinging to the right at the first turn, the way but a few rods from the T, leads directly to Durward's Glen. There one stops by a gate at the left, after crossing a bridge at the bottom a hill.

THE DURWARDS

Bernard I. Durward, a professor, poet, and painter, was born at Montrose, Scotland, and married Margaret Hilyard in the Episcopal church at Manchester, England. They came to America and some time after, at the request of a friend, Joshua Hathaway of Milwaukee, Mr. Durward painted a portrait of Archbishop Henni. While engaged on the picture, the artist was converted to Catholicism. He often remarked that while he got the bishop's picture, the bishop got him. The portrait, with one of Mr. Hathaway, is now in the possession of the State Historical Society of Wisconsin, at Madison.

WISCONSIN WAS A TERRITORY

It was in 1845 that the father, mother, and two sons came from England to Wisconsin, then a territory. They reached Milwaukee without funds but provision for the family was soon assured by an order for a portrait from a merchant in the city. Before making Milwaukee their home, however, the family spent a short time in Dodge County and of this experience a son, Rev. Fr. J. T. Durward, has written:

"Indians being then plentiful and Cooper's tales the popular reading, it was no place for a young wife and children, so he rented a house in Milwaukee; his profession also requiring the more populous locality."

While the family resided in Milwaukee the father painted portraits and occupied the chair of belles lettres in St. Francis seminary. But the ebullitions of life in a city, even the size of Milwaukee, disturbed the artistic mind and the painter sought seclusion in a retreat amongst the Caledonia Hills at the Glen. Like Thoreau, politics, palaces and paved streets had no lure for his aesthetic temperament.

THE CHILDREN

Frederick, afterwards called Bernard, was born in England and died at Riverside, Milwaukee.

Percy, the future artist known as Charles, was born in England and died at the Glen from eating water hemlock. He employed an "o" in his name, spelling it Dorward, the usual form after the so-called reformation. Earlier in Scotch history the name was spelled Durward.

Emerson, afterwards John Thomas, was born in Milwaukee and died in Baraboo in 1918. For many years he had charge of St. Joseph's church in the city, supervised the erection of the present edifice, and wrote a number of books, "Holy Land and Holy Writ," "Durward's Life and Poems," and others.

Emma Theresa, the first daughter, was born and died in Milwaukee. The baby's funeral was by boat and interment was on the Durward property in that city.

Allan, afterwards Rev. James Durward of St. James' Church, St. James, Minnesota, is the owner of the Glen but continues to reside at St. James.

Wilfred J. Durward, taxidermist, photographer, and author of "Annals of the Glen," was born in Milwaukee. For many years his home has been near Tacoma, Washington, where he married in 1919.

CHAPEL AND VIEWS IN THE GLEN

Andrew, born in Milwaukee resides near Tacoma, Washington. His marriage was solemnized in the Glen chapel.

Miss Mary Thecla Durward was born at the Glen and after many years in the state of Washington now calls Baraboo her home.

When the Durward family came from Milwaukee in a one-horse wagon in 1862, crossing the Wisconsin River at Portage, the Glen was reached on November 1, All Saint's Day. Near the trout stream which flows through the Glen and close to the first stepping-stones, is the Maltese Cross cut in the hard sandstone to commemorate their arrival. Just above is the Guardian of the Glen, a bit of art in nature's wild.

WEEPING LEDGE

Continuing up the stream to the boundary of the Glen property, the brook laughs over the projecting stones. Just below is the Weeping Ledge and as the author of "The Annals of the Glen" remarks; "Here one sees that the Glen is indeed

> 'Filled with streams forever weeping,
> Through the rocks in mossy rills.'"

When B. I. Durward led visitors to the spot, especially if there were young ladies in the company, he would roguishly remark: "Bathe your brow at the ledge and you will be ever beautiful." Seldom a miss neglected the opportunity.

ST. MARY'S OF THE PINES

Ascending the hill by a slender path one reaches St. Mary's of the Pines, standing on a knoll. Here occasionally there has been a baptism, a marriage, and a funeral, three important events in the life of man. The chapel was erected by the family, neighbors and friends in 1866.

Two of the sons, James and John, said their first mass here. (James was ordained at Collegeville, Minnesota, and John at St. Francis, Milwaukee.) Charles, the artist, the father and mother, Father John, as well as others have been buried from it, and one son, Andrew, was married here.

The station shrines encircling the chapel and the cemetery are from designs by Delaroche and others. They were painted by Charles, and erected in 1889. Returning from a trip to Palestine that year, Father John brought a little soil from the site of the stations in the Via Dolorosa at Jerusalem, "and this was incorporated in these making this hill-top a veritable Holy Land."

The father, mother, and two sons sleep on the slope in front of the boulder-made church. The inscription for the elder Durward reads:

```
*   * * * * * * * * * * * * * * *   *

*        Bernard I. Durward        *

*               Poet               *

*         Painter, Professor       *

*               Born               *

*          March 26, 1817          *

*               Died               *

*          March 21, 1902          *

*   * * * * * * * * * * * * * * *   *
```

For the mother the following appears:

```
* * * * * * * * * * * * * * * * *
*     Theresa M. Durward      *
*      Mother of Priests      *
*            Born             *
*         Feb. 7, 1821        *
*            Died             *
*        April 22, 1907       *
* * * * * * * * * * * * * * * * *
```

The inscription for the priest reads:

```
* * * * * * * * * * * * * * * * *
*          Beloved           *
*        Father John         *
*            Born            *
*        March 7, 1847       *
*            Died            *
*        Sept. 9, 1918       *
*    He Wrought in Words     *
*    and Builded of Stone    *
*     and by Grace in the    *
*       Hearts of Men.       *
* * * * * * * * * * * * * * * * *
```

A stone for the artist stands at one side, a portion of the inscription reading:

```
* * * * * * * * * * * * * * * * *
*      Charles Dorward       *
*            Born            *
*       Sept. 27, 1844       *
*            Died            *
*        Nov. 12, 1875       *
* * * * * * * * * * * * * * * * *
```

FRESHET IS DISTURBING

When the family first came to the Glen, a little cabin that stood between the bridge, near the spring, and the cliff, was their home. One night a storm arose and the flood of ice, snow and water came pouring through the family shelter. The sleepers were aroused by the onrush and there was much commotion within. As related in "The Annals," one of the urchins, when the lightning flashed, caught sight of the flood from the top of the stair and cried out with pessimistic instinct that afterwards distinguished him:

"O we're all killed, we're all killed."

GUARDIAN ANGEL AT DURWARD'S GLEN

The trap door of the cellar floated open on its hinges, and a confused medley of carrots, beets, onions, and turnips were vomited out, while the rats clung to the grain bags and had to be knocked off into the water.

In this cottage the only daughter, Mary Thecla, was born and in his venerable years the father kept a rose bush growing there to mark the spot.

The family garden was then between the brook and the wooded slope.

THE FOUNTAIN

Ceaselessly flows the fountain by the path across the bridge. This was erected by the poet in memory of his friends and literary heroes. The Christian and Jewish years will be noticed at the base.

The star at the top of the keystone is for Miss Anna Eliza Star, a friend of the family. She resided in Chicago for many years and gave parlor lectures on art.

A de V is for Aubrey Thomas de Vere (1814-1902), the Irish poet and miscellaneous writer. He was a son of Sir Aubrey de Vere, also an Irish poet.

The Greek delta is the nom de plume under which the poet wrote.

On the right, B is for James Booth, a carver and gilder. He was a friend of Mr. Durward in Manchester, England, and later came to New York.

FIRST HOME OF THE DURWARD FAMILY AT THE GLEN

P is for Coventry Kersey Dighton Patmore (1823-1896), the English Catholic poet. He is best known as the author of "The Angel in the House."

Val Zimmerman, represented by the Z, was a merchant friend of the poet in Milwaukee. The sign for his store was the blue flag.

Captain John Nader, Madison, was a civil engineer and under his direction the wingdams along the Wisconsin River were built. He often made trips up and down the stream while supervising the work, frequently visiting the Glen.

VIEW OF THE GLEN

The letter H on the left is for Joshua Hathaway, another civil engineer, who resided in Milwaukee.

He it was who sent the artist-poet to make a portrait of Archbishop Henni.

The stone marked R was placed in memory of John Ruskin.

The remaining stone is for W. J. Onahan, politician and welfare worker of Chicago.

The four basswood trees at the mouth of the Glen, near the Maltese Cross, are often mentioned as the Melzl Quartette, musical friends of the family.

A view of the Potsdam sandstone and basal conglomerate is best obtained by crossing the stepping stones, moving adroitly, if one would not baptise his soles. The rounded pebbles are of quartzite, broken pieces from the Baraboo Mountains of ancient times. Hewing down this wall has been the work of the little trout stream, which has exposed to view the formation left by the waves and action of the Potsdam Sea.

The trout at play in the winding brook and the trees clinging to the fern-clad cliff are interesting sights in this niche of the great outdoors.

The path from the fountain leads to the gallery and low-eaved cottage, the home for many years of the talented family. In the cottage, studio, and gallery the father and sons wrote and painted while the mother made beautiful lace for albs, treasured in many a Catholic church. General Sherman's wife obtained one for her reverend son, Jesuit priest.

Guarding the forest on the crest of the hill to the right is a row of cedars planted in memory of the sons and daughter. Perhaps the Glenman or Glenwoman will tell you about the great Norway spruces of unusual height, about the studio, about "Auld Geordie," the ancient bachelor who gave the disappointing party for the girls of the neighborhood, about the moosewood and other native plants, as well as a word about the feathered visitors that come to the Glen.

CHAPTER XV

SPRING GREEN—TALIESIN—OTHER TRIPS

Spring Green, Helena Shot Tower, and Taliesin—Ableman and Reedsburg—Other Interesting Trips

The journey to Spring Green, Helena, and Taliesin makes a full day's program. From Baraboo the road leads over highway No. 12 to Prairie du Sac then follows the route through Witwen, Black Hawk, over the big hill and down past the Robson farm where there are a number of Indian mounds on the ridge. There is also a road from Sauk City, known as the river road, which passes Lodde's Mill and Cassell Prairie on the way.

After reaching the \village of Spring Green, the road to Helena, the location of the old shot tower, crosses the Wisconsin River and deflects to the left. This shot tower was erected in 1833 as a result of the production of lead in Wisconsin and at the time diverted much of the business from St. Louis to Milwaukee. The enterprise prospered until 1861 when it fell into decay, the land being sold for taxes. Later the location became the site of the Tower Hill Congress and school directed for many years by the late Rev. Jenkin Lloyd Jones of Chicago.

It was here that the American forces crossed the river in the Black Hawk War.

A short distance west of the road which crosses the river near Spring Green is the location of Taliesin, Frank Lloyd Wright's 'love bungalow'. Here on Saturday, August 15, 1914, Julian Carlson, a negro servant, killed seven people with a hatchet, wounding two others. The dead:

Mrs. Mamah Borthwick, a woman, like the owner of the bungalow, with unconventional ideas.

Mrs. Borthwick's son and daughter, John and Martha Cheney, aged 11 and 9 respectively.

Emil Brodelle, aged 30, an architect.

Thomas Brunker, hostler.

Ernest Weston, aged 13.

David Lindblom, gardener.

The injured were William H. Weston and Herbert Fritz, the latter escaping with a broken arm and cuts.

With gasoline the negro set fire to the building and as the occupants attempted to escape through a door and window, one by one, he struck them with a hatchet. The murderer was found in the firebox of the boiler in the basement and died later in the Dodgeville jail as a result of taking muriatic acid soon after committing the crime.

Some of the bodies were burned beyond recognition. "All that was left of her" was buried at Unity Chapel, the Cheney children were cremated in Chicago, the body of Ernest Weston was placed in the Spring Green cemetery, Emil Brodelle was interred in Milwaukee, David Lindblom was lowered in a grave at Unity Chapel and Thomas Brunker sleeps at Ridgeway.

The owner of the property was in Chicago at the time of the tragedy, returning soon after. The building was partly destroyed and later rebuilt along more pretentious lines.

Taliesin was a Cymric bard, whom Welsh legends assign to the 6th century.

Frank Lloyd Wright is an architect of note, having designed the Imperial Hotel in Tokio and other artistic structures.

The return from Spring Green to Baraboo may be made over the scenic route to Plain, thence to Loganville, the County Farm, and Ableman Narrows.

GIBRALTAR BLUFF

Gibraltar Bluff is reached by crossing the Wisconsin River at Prairie du Sac and proceeding along the highway or by leaving the train at the village of Okee and walking a little more than a mile west. Not only does the climb to the top of this imposing eminence give the refreshment and delight bred of an extensive view but the active exercise necessary for the ascent is guaranteed to produce a keen appetite. When the day is fair the climber is rewarded, when he reaches the crest, by a charming outlook which includes a wide expanse of forest, farm and fell, with Lake Wisconsin half-hidden in the distance. The bluff is a well known haunt of the pasque flower or Badger.

The geologists have recently changed the names of some of the formations which are exposed one above the other. The names as given in the "Geology of Wisconsin," Vol. II, 1873-1877, and the more recent ones are as follows:

Old names—

    1. Soil and drift.
    2. Lower Trenton limestone.
    3. St. Peter sandstone.
    4. Lower Magnesian limestone.
    5. Madison sandstone.
    6. Mendota limestone.
    7. Potsdam sandstone.

New names—

    1. Soil and drift.
    2. Black River dolomite.

3. St. Peter sandstone.
4. Lower Magnesian dolomite.
5. Jordan sandstone.
6. St. Lawrence dolomite.
7. Mazomanie sandstone.

PINE HOLLOW

About a mile east of Kings Corners, almost opposite a rural school and cemetery, the buildings of a farmstead appear to hug a fringe of wood, high bluffs forming the sky line in the immediate background of the picture. Leaving the car at the
home of the owner, Walter Welch, a short walk through a grove brings the visitor
against the beetling bluffs; solid, silent, eternities of rock. Pine Hollow is hidden
away from the dust of hooting cars, and is a delightful spot wild and perfect in its
quietude. One may wend his way almost a mile up the sylvan slope along a stream
purling in its rocky channel.

REEDSBURG AND ABLEMAN

A picturesque drive of some forty miles is the one to Reedsburg, the County
Farm, and return. Trunk Line 33 climbs the terminal moraine about a mile west
of Baraboo and from this ice-deposited ridge one obtains an extensive view of the
upper portion of the Baraboo Valley. When the ice blocked the elongated depression between the two ranges of Baraboo Bluffs, a lake filled the cavity between the
hills to the west. Following the retreat of the ice the water cut a gap in the moraine,
draining the area covered by the shallow lake.

As one swings along, occasional glimpses of the Baraboo River is obtained;
rounding a sharp curve a horse-shoe bend is traversed; and two miles farther, at
Ableman, the Upper Narrows of the Baraboo River crowd the sky line. As with the
gorge at Devil's Lake and the one at the Lower Narrows, this was cut by a stream
in ancient geological times, filled with sandstone when the sea intruded, and later
was again eroded. Like the remnant of a drift of snow in the late spring, in the
gorge is a bed of sandstone deposited by the intruding sea. Along the crest on the
opposite side of the river as one rides along, conglomerate may be seen, seeming
almost ready to topple to the base below. The cement pebbles tell of waves beating
on a far-off shore. On the right of the road, near the upper end of the gorge, stands
a picturesque rock resisting the elements, an attractive land mark, carved by the
eternal sculptor.

As Reedsburg is neared, fox farms are passed. The wily animals are grown for
their valuable pelts.

Just after crossing the Baraboo River in Reedsburg, swing to the left, climb
the winding road, coast down to the County Farm, turn to the left, drive across
Narrows Creek Valley, entering Ableman just after passing through the gorgeous
gorge which corresponds in geological history with those of Devil's Lake and the
Baraboo River.

MERRIMACK TO PRAIRIE DU SAC

Take the launch at Merrimack for a river ride to the hydro-electric plant at Prairie du Sac. Down this river went Joliet and Marquette, the first white men in this region, in June, 1673. Duluth and Hennepin were the first to come up the stream in 1680. Down the waterway went a French force in 1727 to erect a Fort on the Mississippi, and along this course retreated, in 1760, the last French garrison of Machinac, seeking the Illinois country.

Other adventures and expeditions have disturbed these waters in times past and in the middle of the last century a procession of rafts plowed southward. Prior to the advent of the railroad a few river steamers dodged the sandbars as often as they could, but today naught but small craft course the stream.

The boatman may show you the location of Rosalietown, near where the river bends southward, a pioneer hamlet of which nothing now remains. The little cemetery has been eaten away by the river.

ANACHER HILL

A vast and pleasing prospect is obtained from Anacher Hill in Caledonia. From Baraboo the elevation may be reached by driving to the Welch Church on Trunk Line Highway 33, going to the right about two miles, to the left a mile and again to the left a mile. The place may also be reached by driving past Pine Bluff or through Dog Hollow.

From the elevation return to the east and west road, then go east about a mile, not descending the bluff. North of the Scherbath home a few rods, the quartzite is seen to outcrop. In the hard rock may be seen a number of pot holes, similar to those at Devil's Lake. As to whether they were made by a waterfall during glacial times or before, geologists have not determined.

A fine view may be obtained from this outcrop or from the land back of the Scherbath house.

Two or three miles west of Anacher hill, a short distance north of the road extending east of Pine Bluff, is another elevation, the Clifford Capener farm, affording a rare outlook.

BAXTER HOLLOW

Baxter Hollow is an extensive wild and rocky valley about a mile west of Kings Corners. Here granite outcrops, there being an excellent exhibit of the sedimentary quartzite resting upon the igneous formation. Wild deer range here and rattlesnakes in abundance creep. Previous to 1920, A. M. Myers killed over 500 in a few years, exhibiting the rattles as truthful trophies of his invasion of the dens of these deadly creatures. In former times trout from the stream filled the creels of many anxious anglers and wildcats were caught by trappers.

THE BARABOO RIVER

Leave the car above the cement bridge between Baraboo and Lyons, and take a launch for a trip on the Baraboo River to North Freedom. If the boatman is a Burroughs he will show you the muskrat glides, the springs, the flowing wells, and the haunts of the wild life.

MERRIMACK TOWARD PORTAGE

From Merrimack a journey may be made up stream, the distance depending on the stage of the water. During the mating season a colony of crows may be seen nesting in the dead trees and in the side of Wild Cat Bluff swallows dwell in unusual number.

LEACH LAKE

About two and one-half miles north of the fair ground, Leach Lake reposes by the road-side. The body of water covers but a few acres and is the source of Leach Creek, famous for cress and trout.

KONKEL'S MILL

About six miles east of Baraboo, Konkel's Mill is hidden away beneath a hill. The stream from the pond escapes through an inviting wood, where the king fisher clatters in his flight and the squirrel chatters in lofty security.

LODDE'S MILL

About three miles west of Sauk City, Lodde's Mill Pond is situated. The rugged bluff and pleasant surroundings attract many visitors. Rare is the day when a number of fishermen are not watching their floats with carking care.

A short distance east of the mill-pond Otter Creek crosses the highway and sinks in the sand, becoming a lost stream.

CEMETERY GROUP OF MOUNDS

There is a fine group of Indian mounds a short distance south of the city, near the east road to Devil's Lake, on the farm owned by W. H. Donald. A bear effigy and others compose the group.

OTHER LITTLE JOURNEYS

This concludes the series of little journeys to be described. Many beautiful ones are omitted, the Hog's Back northwest of Baraboo, many places along the Wisconsin River, and others on the Baraboo Bluffs. By making the twenty-five or more already given, however, one will have acquired a very comprehensive knowledge of Baraboo, Dells, and Devil's Lake region.

Lector House believes that a society develops through a two-fold approach of continuous learning and adaptation, which is derived from the study of classic literary works spread across the historic timeline of literature records. Therefore, we aim at reviving, repairing and redeveloping all those inaccessible or damaged but historically as well as culturally important literature across subjects so that the future generations may have an opportunity to study and learn from past works to embark upon a journey of creating a better future.

This book is a result of an effort made by Lector House towards making a contribution to the preservation and repair of original ancient works which might hold historical significance to the approach of continuous learning across subjects.

HAPPY READING & LEARNING!

LECTOR HOUSE LLP
E-MAIL: lectorpublishing@gmail.com

* 9 7 8 9 3 5 4 2 0 2 5 6 8 *